RAHicks

UNSOLICITED GIFT

UNSOLICITED GIFT

Jacqueline Simms

HARCOURT BRACE JOVANOVICH, PUBLISHERS
San Diego   New York   London

Copyright © 1982 by Jacqueline Simms

All rights reserved. No part of this publication
may be reproduced or transmitted in any form or
by any means, electronic or mechanical, including
photocopy, recording, or any information storage
and retrieval system, without permission in
writing from the publisher.

Requests for permission to make copies of any
part of the work should be mailed to:
Permissions, Harcourt Brace Jovanovich, Publishers,
757 Third Avenue, New York, NY 10017.

Library of Congress Cataloging in Publication Data
Simms, Jacqueline, 1940-
Unsolicited gift.
I. Title.
PR6069.I4134U6   1983   823'.914   83-10684
ISBN 0-15-193079-1

Printed in the United States of America

First American edition

B C D E

CONTENTS

One – Peppercorn Rent
including 'The Memoirs of Miss Fleur'
9

Two – Unsolicited Gift
47

Three – Freelance Rates
65

Four – A Musical Adept
77

Five – Broken Consort
94

Six – Notes from Sumi
111

Seven – Scenes of Childhood
125

Eight – Poste Restante
134

*'I prefer to hear of such unlikely events
As Hermione surviving in private, or
Isabella furnished with a ducal husband . . .'*

ONE

Peppercorn Rent

Greed, in children, is tempered by a sense of justice. One china frog for me (the big shiny one, blue, with bulging eyes), the green one, with a pincushion on its back, for my young sister; she, being more practical, would make better use of it. I lit the candle at night and stared at my frog. It stared back at me, unmoved by my pride of ownership, and it was right, for the very next day it was confiscated. I can't remember what I had done to cause this (I don't say deserve); only the feeling of outrage remains. The frog had been given to me: it was mine. But it remained on the mantelpiece of my grandparents' house, and I could not take it home.

My grandmother eventually paid a peppercorn rent to the owners of the housing estate that grew up where before the pinetrees had crowded round the big, dark house. Perhaps the most likely feeling as one dies will be one of indignation: not yet, this is mine! Hey, just a minute! – It would take too long to explain that it was never yours, and never had been; you had hardly moved in.

Was someone watching from the woods? I didn't consider this seriously at the time. The paths led fairly easily round the edges, and criss-crossed systematically so that trees could be felled, the undergrowth contained, and fircones gathered. The bamboo grove could be plundered for bows and arrows and bitter snacks between meals. The oak tree nearer the house provided acorn-cup pipes in which we smoked, or at least smouldered, dried grass and moss. We gasped and coughed under the huge branches. Why then the sense of suspense, as if someone, snatching peeps between his fingers, was counting, faster and faster, up to ten? Would it be cheating to hide inside the house? My heart pounded as I crouched behind the dusty curtains that covered the piles of trunks and hat boxes on the landing. The hunting cries in the garden grew more plaintive.

I don't mean to suggest that my grandmother believed she had a right to anything. On the contrary, she was entirely modest. Her story might have been written by Charlotte Brontë: an orphan, a poor relative, she was first sent away to school, and then became a governess in France to the children of a wicked employer, who was having an affair with a Count; my grandmother had to run the gauntlet of their interrupted passion as she passed through the salon to and from her bedroom. In this household she met my grandfather, a distant relation of the family, at that time an earnest student of chemistry at one of a series of European universities. It is certain that everything she received she felt she held in trust, or rather, she gave herself back to it, so that by the end of her life you could not distinguish her from her gentle surroundings. Her smell was of the dried rose leaves in her drawing-room; her delicate skin reflected the translucence of the watery light in her conservatory; if you had been so intrepid as to touch with the tip of your tongue her cheek, or one of her thin fingers, you would have found she tasted of fine brown bread-and-butter, lavender, and curiously, of the rather stale but fragrant coffee that she served from a samovar-type coffee pot. It is only possible to half-fix her movements – she was insubstantial – but I think I can see her sitting at her Louis Quinze desk whose pigeon holes held numerous little notebooks with pencils attached to them by coloured cord, or moving around the conservatory with a watering can.

Later, even later than the period of the peppercorn rent, she had to leave her house and go to a Home where, unrecognizable, divorced from everything that had given her smell, and colour, and taste, she crumbled to dust through our busy fingers.

Should nothing, then, have remained? It is surprising that the confidence of so many Victorian Trusts and Deeds of Settlement should have left us with any doubts on this matter! Certainly my parents have looked after the inheritance well, if anything too well, but the habit of life is lost. The spidery cracks that I used to run my fingers down are carefully concealed with a matching filler; the pale rings left by the bases of china bowls filled with the dried rose leaves are polished until they barely glimmer below the lustrous surfaces. Nothing stands on the inherited pieces. How much better it would have been to burn everything that belonged to my grandparents on a pyre after their death. We could still have found among the by then scanty woods enough fircones to start the blaze. Instead, under the complacent eyes of the Trustees, the possessions were valued, and sorted, and distributed in equal shares to the next generation who in turn would polish and insure them, in order to pass them on, their value intact, to the next.

But like my grandmother, once out of context the possessions lost their sense of themselves. Let's look at them, as they retrace in the paste-filled cracks of their consciousness their eventful history. The Louis Quinze desk began, naturally enough, in France, entrusted with the discreet confidences of a lady-in-waiting to the French Queen. True, it had to emigrate to London in a hurry to avoid the bonfires of the Revolution, but eventually it made its way home to the Rue du Faubourg St Honoré, where it was restored with relief to its elegant surroundings. The English climate would never really suit it. During the mid-nineteenth century it studied music at second hand. Placed out of the sunlight behind the keyboard of the grand piano, it had an excellent view of the repertoire my great-grandmother was playing, and took part eagerly in her lessons with a famous conductor. But, wait a minute, that must have been when they were for a while in Munich. For it was there – and now the desk enters Musical History – that one day a message was delivered to the house of the music student to await the arrival of the teacher. The message read (the desk must be forgiven for knowing this, since the note lay on its surface for some time) – I translate: 'Goodbye, Hans. I have gone to Richard.' The signature: 'Cosima'. But the desk, which preferred the French music of its youth, although it had listened courteously to illustrated discussions of the *leitmotif*, would not have dwelt on this.

From early on, then, the desk's life would never be quite the same again. It continued to travel widely, now in the care of the music student's son (the piano, when the music student no longer played, waited in store until there was a house big enough to hold it, and possibly another music student to play it), while he pursued his chemical studies and met my grandmother. And she in turn received the desk with the rest of the furniture into the house my grandfather built for her, where she shared with it both the English climate and her sweet and reticent nature.

That was where I first saw them, and there was never any question in my mind as to their right to be there. Nor did their bearing suggest they presumed on the place or time where they found themselves. How could they be blamed for the need to change the rules? No legislator can look with equanimity into the eyes of the old. The new envelopes would be too large for the pigeon holes of the Louis Quinze desk, the telephone too wide to stand on its narrow top. What shall we do with our ill-fitting envelopes? Where do we store the waiting desk? Can we live with the look in its eyes? When it burns, will we choke on the fumes from our acorn-cup pipes?

Only a child would ask so many questions.

You may want to ask me one more: well, am I? Am I sitting at the Louis Quinze desk as I write about it? But I have said that if ever it arrived, in a great packing case, its black lacquered corners carefully padded, its slim legs wrapped round like a dancer's, I should not know where to put it! The action of a typewriter would shake it to pieces in a single letter to the insurance agent; I had no intention of typing that letter. But it is not as simple as that, for you must have realized that I loved the Louis Quinze desk, which began in France two hundred years ago, and eventually belonged to my grandmother, after which I felt its useful life was over.

It is not easy to live with a genius. I'm not sure how most people reach that conclusion; perhaps they have picked up the pieces after the genius has dispersed them. Grandmother, who lived with a genius, would never have said such a thing. The point about a genius is not that he is troublesome to have around, but that on the whole he is not around. Absence, of mind and body, is his main characteristic. Or rather, to modify that, he is conspicuously absent when he is needed in the normal course of events, but then unnaturally evident when it is inconvenient; he may stay up working to all hours of the night, for instance, combining absence and evidence in a peculiarly distressing manner. I use the male pronoun, by the way, not out of an old-fashioned sense of rightness, or even statistical likelihood, but simply because in this story the genius is a grandfather.

By the time I knew grandfather, his genius had dimmed; it guttered gently, like the gas lights we sat under in the evenings. The house was dark not only because of the economy in artificial lighting, combined with the stained panelling, the Germanic still-lifes of slaughtered game, and the pinetrees that came up too close to the window in order to remind grandfather of the Black Forest of his youth. It was also dark with Thought. Thought overhung everything, heavy and dust-laden like the velvet curtains I hid behind on the landing.

The more obvious traces of Thought were to be found in grandfather's study. Here an enormous desk, that could have swallowed the Louis Quinze desk at one gulp, took up half the room. Ponderous leather-bound books filled the glass-fronted shelves and piled up in heaps on the floor. Grandfather took a delight in opening these tomes to show me their impenetrably black Gothic lettering. Other books, paperbound, with ragged edges and paler, more graceful typefaces were, he told me, French *romans*: happily they too contributed to Thought. When my grandfather said 'French' his eyes grew distant and tender, and he looked up at the portrait on the wall above the fireplace, where the red-headed, straight-nosed music student – his mother – gazed sternly south, perhaps towards Germany and the unfortunate Hans von Bülow.

Grandfather was a mystery. He spoke fluently seven languages, including two dead ones. Sometimes in the evenings the family would persuade him to recite from memory. He would smile to himself behind his little moustache, appear to withdraw into the recesses of a European library, and then – but what was it? What language? In what mighty style did he declaim to us? What did it all mean? If only I could recognize it even now! Dostoevsky, Voltaire, Goethe? But, 'That was Greek,' whispered my mother.

It is hard for a grandson to see the inconveniences of an elderly genius, who now has time at his disposal to be benign and affectionate. Grandmother could have told us more, but she would rather not, so who am I to exaggerate the nuisance value of domesticity, and especially of his own children, to a genius? Quite early on grandfather built a laboratory where he could conduct and even sleep over his experiments without upsetting the controlled running of a household. Explosions, and the accompanying expletives, the frustrations that dog the remorseless advance of science, took their rightful place at the far end of the garden.

The name that attached itself to the family in Germany, and that eventually reached the home counties (calling *en route* on the music student and the Louis Quinze desk in Paris), was to cause trouble for the next generation, which had to fight in the British streets to defend its newly-naturalized honour. There can be no peace for the heirs of men with liberal views, particularly when a foreign name is combined with a laboratory devoted to explosive experiments at the end of a wooded garden. But a compromise was reached some time after the First World War, when the umlaut was tactfully abandoned on local invoices, although it remained in meticulous evidence on the fly-leaves of the thoughtful leather volumes.

In the same way that it was impossible to cherish the umlaut, it is proving difficult now to maintain an equivocal tone while referring to those early experiments. With each explosion, the modern age came nearer, for while the curiosity and speculation that drove grandfather's private genius was no different in kind from that which produced the wheel or the first printing press (whose heirs were to print so many important scientific papers), the implications for the first time began to escape even the geniuses who demonstrated them. No one, not even grandmother, begged grandfather to stop, though many suppers were ruined, and the parish hummed with rumours of spying and sabotage. Grandfather himself, however, in a gesture of some refinement, refused to be paid for his contribution to the right side of the war effort.

But science is no respecter of genius, nor of refinement, and already a mere change in direction was leading him, in a proper spirit of scientific detachment, to conclude his experiments whose use was superseded. Thus it was that, while electronic theory took over from chemical theories of the conversion of mass into energy, in the process it converted the life of my grandparents, until domestic fission became a thing of the past. And so grandfather closed his laboratory, and returned to the house to play with his grandchildren. Q.E.D.

While I was poring over the large volumes in grandfather's study, my sister Fleur was almost certainly with grandmother in the conservatory. Excuse me, grandfather, while I check. Yes, she is at this very minute dipping the long-spouted watering can into the deep cool well ... If Fleur could read this, she would probably say it was not that she had a natural affinity with flowers, but simply that since I was usually with grandfather she felt it incumbent on her to keep grandmother company — and grandmother usually happened to be in the conservatory.

My young sister was born in 1938, when I was three. I remember looking at her cautiously over the edge of her crib. Her fist was tightly clenched against the world and perhaps, I thought, against me. I extended a finger and her hand opened and closed on it automatically. The next few years must have been devoted to growing, because it is not until she is about seven years old that Fleur jumps out of the crib into my memory and begins her life in earnest.

The idea that brought her to my attention must have come to her at one of the interminable lunches we sat through on our visits to our grandparents. Meals in those days – despite post-war stringencies – lasted for hours. First came the rounding-up of the family from the corners of the house and garden. The children, who had been hanging round the kitchen door for at least half an hour, were being sent to wash their hands for the second time and in turn to retrieve the missing adults. But slowly the instinct that turns all animals' heads troughwards at certain times of the day would prevail, and the family would at last assemble in the dining-room.

Here there was a shifting of chairs to suit the tall and the short, the piling-up of cushions for the smaller children, the surreptitious swapping of favourite silver dessert spoons. Next, in the absence of the saying of Grace, came an awkward moment of hesitation, quickly dispelled by a flourish of napkins and the clearing of throats that introduced the discussion as to the language in which lunch might be held. But it seems that the blushes of the grandchildren and the inadequacies of the middle generation would soon prevail over grandfather's sense of the propriety of French as a gastronomic accompaniment, and return the table with relief to the local tongue.

The soup endured formalities of this kind. But as the bowls were carried away to the hatch and the covered vegetable dishes began to arrive at the table, the children to swing their legs and drop their cutlery, the great topic, second only to the War in family conversation, would be ushered in. For it was only to the clatter of the 'Breaking of the Trust' that the appetites of the adults could be satisfied. This subject of subjects was carved with the joint, served with the vegetables, passed around with the salt, and poured with the gravy. During dessert it briefly sweetened, only to return in all its flavour with the tang of the home-made cheese. By then the children had long since given up any attempt at distraction, and rested all their remaining hopes of entertainment on grandmother's final act with the bubbling coffee pot, whose silver tap turning this way and that poured streams of piping hot coffee into the little cups.

When Fleur had been allowed to turn the tap for the last time, she beckoned to me and slithered to the floor from the heap of cushions. I paused to ask if we could get down, and we were waved vaguely away.

'Have a fag,' said Fleur, as I joined her in our oak-tree hideout. She sat cross-legged against the trunk and puffed furiously at a straw stem. These had replaced acorn-pipes in our rituals for the time being, as real smoke poured down the hollow funnels into our throats. She passed the stem to me; I passed it back. Our eyes streamed.

'What shall we do?' I asked, when I could speak again.

And she explained her idea. I said I hadn't noticed Fleur in the intervening years since she grasped my finger in her crib, but that isn't really accurate. She was always, from the moment she could talk, full of plans. It usually took me to help her bring them about: I would climb the tree, make the bows from the thickest bamboo canes, carry on the baskets when she auctioned the fircones, or break the window at the far end of the deserted laboratory so we could get in; and I often took the blame, as I was older and a boy. But it was Fleur who master-minded our campaigns.

Today she announced that we should get married and make a Will, and leave everything to our children, so that no one else, least of all the new Government, could get it.

'Don't be silly. Brothers and sisters can't get married,' I said dubiously.

'Why not?'

I couldn't think why not.

'We're too young to have children anyway. And where would we keep them?'

'In the laboratory.'

I thought the laboratory was too dusty for new children, and it smelt horribly of ancient chemicals. Fleur saw it would be a good idea to approach the question from another angle.

'Don't you want to get everything?' she demanded.

'What everything?'

'The things. The furniture, the money. The house even.'

'I suppose so.'

'Well, if we're married we can inherit it, have children, and pass it on to them when we die.'

It was beginning to sound like lunch all over again.

'We can keep it in the family,' persisted Fleur.

And eventually I agreed.

Fleur and I were married a year after the end of the War. She was nearly eight and I was eleven, and should have known better. On the morning of our wedding I got up early and carved the date on the thickest branch of the oak tree. We gave one another wedding presents after breakfast. Fleur gave me one of the little notebooks with a pencil on a coloured cord, which she said grandmother had given her, and I gave her a necklace I had made from threaded acorns and cowrie shells. She said we should not speak to one another again until the wedding service, which was to take place after lunch in the laboratory. I think I spent the morning with grandfather, and at lunchtime we sat studiously at opposite ends of the table and ignored one another. I was beginning to feel rather frightened. As we left the dining-room I suggested to her casually that we might postpone it:

'Wouldn't it be nicer to have a summer wedding?'

'It's too late. You've carved the date. Don't talk to me, it's unlucky!' hissed Fleur.

I could, I suppose, have jilted her, but most bridegrooms who jilt their intended brides do not have to live with the injured party in the same house. I resolved to go along with the ceremony. I could always draw the line at later developments.

It was a rationalist household, but a Book of Common Prayer was kept for reference and use at certain social celebrations. This I borrowed for the occasion of my marriage, and now stood awaiting the arrival of the bride in the darkest corner of the laboratory. Fleur appeared punctually. She wore a wreath of daisies on her head and carried a posy which I recognized as coming from the flower vase in the morning-room. She looked pretty for her, as she stood quietly and solemnly by my side.

'Dearly beloved,' I read to the retorts and balances in the laboratory, 'we are gathered together in the sight of God, and in the face of this congregation, to join together this man and this woman in holy Matrimony . . .' When it came to the questions, Fleur said 'Wilt thou have me, Fleur, to thy wedded wife' and I said 'Wilt thou have *me*, Michael, to thy wedded husband', and we both answered 'I will'. And we gave our troth to each other in this manner: Fleur took my hand, and I put upon the fourth finger of her left hand a ring; it was a curtain ring that I had taken from the kitchen drawer, and it gleamed in the dusky light of the laboratory. 'Is it real gold?' Fleur couldn't help whispering.

I skipped the rest of the Service until the Lesson that is read in the absence of a sermon, and that I read, very slowly, in full. Fleur sat down on the floor and listened to me gravely on the subject of the duty of husbands towards their wives and wives towards their husbands: 'For this cause shall a man leave his father and mother, and shall be joined unto his wife; and they two shall be one flesh. This is a great mystery . . . Husbands, love your wives, and be not bitter against them . . . Whose adorning, let it not be that outward adorning of plaiting the hair, and of wearing of gold . . . but let it be the hidden man of the heart . . .' I closed the book. My wedding had made me feel quite tired.

'Should I not wear my ring then?' asked Fleur, when the Service seemed to be over.

'Oh, I think you're allowed to wear that one,' I said.

'And I've got plaits!'

'It's against Vanity, that's all,' I said, rather embarrassed. 'So long as you don't show off about them . . .'

'I see,' said the newly-wedded wife, and she slipped her hand meekly into mine.

The piano that had been in store by the end of the previous century, at some cost to its condition, had by now for many years lived in my grandparents' house, where most recently by common consent it had been earmarked for Fleur, of all of us the most promising successor to the music student. 'Have you shut the piano, Fleur?' would be the last words she heard as she went up to bed, and since she was the only person likely to have opened it, this did not seem an unreasonable enquiry.

Each year she would oversee the annual call of the piano tuner. The tuner, who was blind, born, as he would always remind us, in the same decade as the piano, would arrive in a suit as black and shiny as the instrument itself. He enquired after Fleur's studies, and she would play her latest piece, if only to demonstrate to him the sad need for his visit. Then I heaved open the main lid and held it with arms braced and trembling, calling 'quick, quick!' as Fleur manoeuvred the prop into position, ready for the tuning to begin. While the piano tuner slowly and painstakingly struck the same note again and again and gave little tweaks to the stiff pegs, we would lean over the edge of the piano and sniff at its reverberating and musty interior. A fine white dust had fallen through the strings from the lavender bags and moth balls that were stored inside to keep the felts from deteriorating even further. But between the third and fourth octave, when he was brought a cup of tea and a plate of shortbread biscuits (which he insisted on sharing with us), the piano tuner would shake his head and advise Fleur that the felts were already too far gone, and that as her technique developed she would very soon need another piano, one with the modern action that had come in around the turn of the century, although admittedly it did not do the same for Brahms. By midday the apotheosis of the tuning would approach. Released from his craning and attentive position over the strings, the tuner now sat back peacefully and, his blind eyes oblivious of his hands, searching only for the notes stored in his head, he would play to us the Intermezzo that he had performed, in household after household, perhaps daily, for the past fifty years.

Although in the daytime grandfather cultivated my company, especially when he detected in me a latent interest in his long dormant chemical research, in the evening, as he moved from the study to the drawing-room, Fleur became the object of his affectionate attention. He would ask her to play (but would hear nothing against the quality of the piano on which his mother had played to him when, as a small boy, he had hung around her). Now it was Fleur whom grandfather allowed to linger with him until the gong sounded for dinner. Sometimes even then, evading the reproaches of the more intolerant adults, he would come upstairs between courses to say a proper goodnight, to see which books we were reading, and to receive from Fleur a kiss on each of his dry cheeks.

'Goodnight, goodnight!' we called excitedly as we lay down and quickly pulled the blankets up to our noses, distracted already by the retreating candle shadows and the thought of the darkness that would swoop down on us as he departed.

'Goodnight *who*?' retorted Grandfather, a stickler for European form until the last.

'Goodnight, Grand*pa*.'

In the early months of our marriage Fleur did not appear to develop her theories of property and inheritance in great detail, although we had every chance to learn from the debate of our seniors which raged on around us whenever they assembled. But one day at Easter, perhaps a year after our wedding, she spun her ring at me as we passed in the hall, in the sign that meant we were to meet, man and wife, as soon as possible. Our married status had fluctuated: weeks would go by, especially during school terms, when I almost forgot about it. But then, with this cryptic signal, Fleur would recall us to our vows. Today when she spun her ring I felt none of the reluctance I had felt as a younger child when she summoned me, but instead a queer and fatalistic resolution. And so I went at once, by a devious route, to the laboratory.

It was our first visit to the laboratory since the summer holidays the previous year. The broken window was overgrown with ivy which I tugged aside and, because I too had grown, I had to break some more glass before I could squeeze through. A mixture of cobwebs and rain had spread a thin layer of mud over the working tops and floor inside. The same strong smell of chemicals, perhaps tinged with gas from the still connected burners, filled the room, which was mustier and shabbier than ever. By now I had started chemistry lessons at school, and I noticed for the first time how well stocked were the racks of glass tubes and retorts, read the names on the jars, and wondered how I could ask grandfather about them without letting him guess that we had been in the laboratory. The wicks of the candles we stored there were damp, and it took several matches to get one alight. I was wedging it carefully between the floorboards when I heard Fleur climbing through the window.

Fleur had been a square, rosy little girl. Now she had become thinner and paler. She still wore plaits, but they were rather weedy-looking, as if they had begun to outgrow their strength; when she played the piano she would toss them fiercely over her shoulders to get them out of her way. Her movements were as definite as ever. She jumped easily down from the window sill and came and crouched beside me, as I tried to light the second candle.

'It is time we did something,' she said eventually, when the second candle was lit and flickering unsteadily beside the other one.

I think if she had said this at any time before, I would have been too frightened. I would have put her off, and found an excuse to go back to the house. But now I knew what she meant, and that there was no way out, so I looked at her boldly.

'Yes, I know,' I said. 'Husbands, love your wives, and be not bitter against them.'

Fleur cleared a space on the floor and dusted it with her handkerchief. Then she lay down on her back and waited for me while I took off my heavy scout belt, and emptied my pockets of stones and gadgets. I lowered myself over her very carefully, and dipped down and up a few times above her still and straight body, making sure I did not let my weight fall on her. And in this way our marriage was first consummated.

From now on we would meet nearly every day in the holidays and go through the same silent formalities. Fleur lay motionless; I took off my belt and emptied my pockets, and dabbed at her gently. But afterwards, she would jump up briskly and dismissively and proceed to a new and crucial phase of the plan. She had begun to draw up a contract between us, which would, she said, enable us to make a mutual Will and Testament. Her theory was that we should mark out for ourselves the things we most wanted in our grandparents' house and then leave them to one another. We spent hours discussing the furniture, the books, and the paintings, and in the house we would pass things with a confirming nod: 'Yours' or 'Mine'. I wrote it all down in two columns headed Assets, in the little notebook Fleur had given me for a wedding present.

'But what if they break the Trust before we are ready?' I asked her from time to time.

'They won't be ready for years,' said Fleur. 'They'll talk and talk, and by the time they decide what to do, everything will belong to us anyway!'

We divided most of the Assets painlessly; Fleur was quite happy for me to have the books; I with a magnanimous gesture gave her the Louis Quinze desk, and she gave me the piano and the portrait of the music student. Only once was there a problem, and that was in the case of the two china frogs. I of course chose my gleaming blue frog, that had been so unjustly taken away from me the day after it was given, but suddenly I saw that in my Will I would lose it again, though only to Fleur this time.

'I'd like to keep my frog,' I said obstinately. 'And I don't want the other one, so you needn't leave it to me.'

Fleur was very angry. She saw in this the fatal flaw that would jeopardize our pact. At last she persuaded me that the best solution was the obvious one: I must let her choose the blue frog for the time being, but only in order that she might leave it to me, the rightful beneficiary. I eventually accepted this, but the argument had very slightly undermined our mutual confidence. After that Fleur referred to my frog with a sardonic note in her voice as '*your*-my frog'. I was too old to care much about the silly frog any more, but I grew hot and bothered; I told myself it was the principle of the thing.

As grandfather grew older, fell ill, and eventually took to his bed, he seemed to depend increasingly on my company. During the holidays I would spend hours perched on the edge of his high bed, trying to answer his questions about the way science was being taught in school these days. If I complained about the routine drudgery of chemistry, he would do his best to help me make the connections that were always missing in the classroom. In this way, he not only tried to teach me the value of patient observation – no scientist can be in a hurry – but also gave me a glimpse of the imaginative leaps that must to some extent precede drudgery, and are perhaps the only thing that make it bearable. I began to understand a little about his own work, and to appreciate his resistance to the hypothesis which, although presented early in the century, he rightly argued had not been conclusively proved until many years later. I did not quite see then it was not only scientific rigour that held my grandfather back, but also, surely, a reluctance to admit the implications for his own line of research which had, as it were, reached a provincial railway junction: from this point the express train would run to the capital. Not knowing that I had long since made myself at home in his laboratory, he one day gave me the key and told me to fetch one of the balances. I had already polished the balance he described and set it up on my bench, although I did not know how to use it. I brought it to his bedroom and listened carefully as he explained its delicately adjusted mechanism.

When our talks tired him he would lie back with his eyes

shut and sometimes, as I waited, he would appear to be trying to recite to himself from the formulae that filled his laboratory exercise books. During one of our last talks, perhaps sensing my growing comprehension, he warned me not to think of using the laboratory until I knew exactly what was involved. He seemed worried for the first time that he had not disposed of its contents. I hastily did my utmost to reassure him; I didn't want the adults invading our sanctum and putting a stop to my harmless glass-working experiments. Perhaps it was now, too, that he told me himself about his work for the war effort in 1914–18, when, in America, he had helped manufacture explosives to be fired against his country of origin. (Only three years before our talk, the main line of research had contributed to even greater disaster.)

'At least you weren't *paid* for it, Grandpa,' I quoted glibly.

Before we came home for Christmas, grandfather died, and the discussions between the adults entered a period of intense upheaval. For with the passing of the older generation (my grandmother's future seemed to be taken care of in a way that didn't affect the new decisions), the onus fell on the middle generation to come to a swift and responsible conclusion. By the following spring, rumour was rife that the Trust was indeed to be broken. Fleur and I now proceeded, with the help of glimpses of grandfather's Will (a copy of which lay quite openly in the old study), to the drawing up of our own mutual Will and Testament. I must admit that by now I felt sceptical about our plans, but Fleur was undeterred. At supper one night she even went so far as to ask our father what he planned to do with everything when he had broken the Trust. He said in a surprised way, 'Nothing special! Go on looking after it, of course. Why, have you got your eye on something?' and laughed easily. Fleur blushed with annoyance, and changed the subject. But this reassured her that the breaking of the Trust might prove more meaningless in practice than I suggested. She felt our father would honour its terms in the spirit if not out of legal necessity.

But by now it was clear to me that something was different. The Assets were coming to have a more random attachment: they might or might not remain; they could or could not belong to us in the future. For the first time I began to doubt whether everyone else would understand that they were really ours. Gradually everything took on the provisional and nerve-racking status that previously I had associated with my frog. Perhaps Fleur sensed this too, as she put the last touches to the Will and Testament. Her language grew more forcible; I was called upon to check the spelling of every legal flourish. Father came across me reading for the tenth time a tournure in grandfather's Will.

'I can see you are hoping to come into a fortune,' he remarked drily, and after that the Will was nowhere to be found. Perhaps he feared the effect of presumptive riches on the character of the younger generation.

But very little seemed to change in the couple of years that followed grandfather's death. Grandmother remained in the house, and discussions about her future were vague. Once we were alarmed by the visit of a surveyor who had been asked to value the buildings and surrounding woodland (Fleur watched him angrily as he paced round the laboratory). But he went away, and we heard no more about it. In the holidays Fleur and I fell compulsively back into our silent ritual behaviour, although more and more I could not relate it to my life elsewhere. I was fifteen and Fleur was twelve when she again suggested that our contract must move into a more decisive phase. I was examining one of grandfather's notebooks in the laboratory, trying to master his private shorthand and check certain measurements against the contents in the jars, and not really concentrating when she said, in the distant way in which she always referred to our vows, that it was time we took the next step. At first I thought she merely meant we must proceed to the signing and witnessing of the Will which, at least on my part, out of boredom with the whole project we still had not done.

'Oh, yes, any time,' I answered carelessly. I had managed to pull out one of the tight stoppers, and was sniffing at an unidentified acrid liquid. 'But who shall we get to witness it? We can hardly ask Mary, or a member of the family!'

'Oh, that,' said Fleur. 'Yes, we must do that too, I suppose. No, I mean we must make sure of the future. We must be able to pass on our Inheritance. We are old enough now.'

'You mean?' I put the jar back on the shelf and stared at her.

'Yes,' said Fleur. 'We must, we always intended to.'

'Oh no, I don't think we did,' I interrupted. 'In fact, I know I didn't . . .'

'Yes, you did. It's in the Will: "and to our son and heir . . ."'

'Oh, that! I was joking. Anyway, it's not signed.' I laughed treacherously.

'We must try,' she insisted. 'I can have a baby now.'

'But you don't understand. You must be mad! Don't you know anything? We mustn't. You might *have* a baby!' I babbled wildly. I had begun to shiver in the stuffy laboratory.

'Don't be silly. Of course,' she said. 'It will be ours', and she put her hand on my belt.

Once more I took off my scout belt and emptied my pockets, and when I turned round I saw that she had taken off her clothes. 'Fleur, are you sure?' I said, as I took a step towards her, but she only smiled at me. So this time I lay heavily on her; and Fleur, who had always been brave as a little girl, cried.

From that day on I grew bitter against my sister. We met without explanation in the laboratory, and afterwards she would go away and I would continue my work on the chemicals. I cleaned out the rest of the burners, and began to set up one of grandfather's more minor experiments. In the house I avoided her, and she made no attempt to spend time with me. I was morose with the family, and rough with Fleur when she came to the laboratory. I didn't ask her whether her plan was being fulfilled; I didn't want to know. I couldn't connect the part of me that shivered and lay down on the floor of the laboratory with the part that stood experimenting at the work tops. Fleur did not mean to cry again in my presence, but one afternoon, as I crossed the landing from my bedroom, I heard a curious scuffling sound from behind the curtains that covered the boxes and cases. I stopped to listen, wondering if it was mice, or even another bird that had come down the landing chimney and was now panicking in the dark. I tapped on a case and listened, and the sound stopped on an indrawn breath. Perhaps for a whole minute we waited in silence for the other to speak, then Fleur said 'Go away'. Why did I not disobey her then? If I had pulled back the curtain and pushed my way through the boxes to her, nothing would have been the same. But I said nothing; and Fleur had said nothing when we parted at the end of the holidays to go back to our separate schools. I dreaded the next holidays, and managed to arrange to go away on a school expedition instead of going straight home. So I did not see my sister for nearly four months.

HERE BEGINNETH THE MEMOIRS OF MISS FLEUR
(as Mary calls me). By Herself, in her Thirteenth Year.

Mary put ideas into my head, and so she deserves to have a say in the title of my Memoirs, which I am beginning at school at the end of the summer term. She never stops talking. As fast as carrot scrapings and potato peel fly from her knife, words pop out of her mouth. 'You should have seen this, you should have heard that' she says; and she has more relations than everyone in the Old Testament put together. But she can't help noticing that she isn't married, and this makes her very sad. Sometimes there's a great silence at the end of the peeling. Then she throws the last potato into the pan, and bangs the pan on to the stove, and the bang says clearly 'And Mary begat No One'. None of her relations is what she calls close. At Christmas, Mary says, only close relations count. She usually goes to her uncle's family for Christmas dinner (that's at lunchtime), but really she feels she should be looking after her own son. 'He'd be nearly your age by now, Miss Fleur,' she says with a sniff.

'It might have been a girl, you know,' I say rattily, but Mary doesn't seem to hear. The truth is, Mary's secret is, she had a young man once, but he was killed early in the War. They had done it, once, before he went away, and Mary nearly had a baby! It took me ages to understand this, as she wouldn't tell me any details. When I was little I thought perhaps the young man was meant to have brought the baby back from somewhere (though it seemed unlikely they'd want one from Germany). Anyway, Mary's baby stopped before it was even born, so she still convinces herself it was a boy. After that she kept herself to herself in memory of her young man, and that's why she still peels potatoes and carrots in my grandmother's house.

I tried to get Mary to tell me more about her young man – where did they do it, for instance? – but it was no good. She showed me a picture of him in his uniform, and he looked just like an ordinary boy; he looked no older than Michael does now! I was amazed he could be a soldier, let alone a proper young man.

'You must keep yourself for the right person, Miss Fleur.' She always ended our talks like this. 'It doesn't do to be disappointed.' In those days the whole idea made me want to laugh, but nor could I imagine waiting around indefinitely, so I didn't say much to Mary about my future prospects. She'd have been surprised to learn, for instance, that Master Michael and Miss Fleur were already married.

So would Miss X, my headmistress. If only I could tell her even now! I should like to break the news just as the Vicar shakes hands with her on the church steps after Sunday morning service, while the choir files out under her eyes. I could step out of line (it wouldn't be too surprising for me, as a one-time server, to want to pay my respects to the Vicar), and 'Good morning, Vicar,' I'd say politely. He would forget my name as usual: 'Good morning, er . . .' 'Fleur,' would say Miss X hastily, perhaps a little teeny bit worried already.

'I've just stepped over to tell you I'm married,' I'd say. 'To whom, dear?' would ask the Clerical Codfish, before he could stop himself, and before he saw Miss X's face beginning to turn a horrible hue.

'To my brother, who else?' I'd reply. 'That was an interesting sermon you preached this morning, dear Vicar.' And off I'd go.

I know the Vicar disapproves of me; he would prefer boys to be servers. Our headmistress impressed on us that it was a great honour for a few chosen girls to be allowed to serve. 'Of course, when you reach a certain age, you may not continue,' she said. 'And the Vicar would never have considered you at all if there were boys available.' She looked sharply at me as she said this, since she believes my besetting sin is Pride. Perhaps she thought I would notice and resent the implications of this somehow conditional state of grace.

Well, last term I did reach a certain age, rather sooner than expected (at least, sooner than I had expected), and so fell from the state of grace. I am no longer a server. But all the time I was, I was married.

In fact I miss the freedom of that privilege. It seems so odd that I was allowed to wander about at seven in the morning quite alone, when later in the day, even to go and buy some sweets, I would have to be 'in the company of four girls'. It must be something to do with the server's white veil: I was untouchable! At 7 a.m. everyone else was asleep, and absolutely no one knew where I was once I had left the House. Of course, they knew I was on my way to church, but the point is I might not have been: I could have crossed the road and run in the opposite direction. I could even have caught a train, and met Michael (if he could have been persuaded to sneak out of his school; we are only thirty miles apart). But I didn't think of any of these things at the time, though I took as long as I could over my solitary walk to church.

By the end of the service, I usually had rather a headache from the strings of the veil, which tugged the hair at the back of my neck. I can't be bothered to describe how dreadfully mortifying those early morning services were – how the bell rope nearly pulled my arms out of their sockets as it flopped wildly out of control; how the Vicar monopolized the mirror in the vestry, just when I was trying to re-tie my veil; how he gabbled his responses, aiming the poor mutilated words at me like so many low-slung hard balls: 'Whoosh, slap!', ignoring my slow, looping returns and dignified 'Amens'; how he swilled and gulped as he washed up after Communion (though I tried not to listen as I slid the silver lid of the wafer box over the ranks of wafers, smooth as tiddlywinks). 'The blessing of God . . .' he would say at last, angrily, as his hand flew through the air above my head . . .

I miss too the smell of the wisps of sweet waxy smoke that drifted up to the rafters when I snuffed the candles, before I hurried back to school for breakfast.

Miss X says Pride is the worst of the Seven Deadly Sins, and that it is, inevitably, my besetting sin. It is the worst because it contains all the others, or so she says. Yet I am sure that if she really knew which was my besetting sin she would be far more shocked. I doubt that she has properly appreciated Lust in the girls whose spiritual well-being she has taken into her charge (with due reference to the Vicar). That may sound as if I am rather above it all, rather removed, but that's because I am twelve and a half, and really do feel a bit past it by now. I've been married since I was seven; my marriage was formally consummated when I was nine (when Michael was, I think, still a little ignorant), and properly last holidays, after my fall from the state of grace. Until I wrote it down here, I haven't told anyone, except my friend Jane. In fact, when Michael (who is sixteen now) and I did it properly for the first time, although it was my idea, I hated it. That's another thing that has made me feel differently about Lust. It wasn't, to tell you the truth, what I had expected. I don't think I expected, for instance, to feel anything; it hurt, which I hadn't imagined at all. I think if I had been prepared for that, it would have been different. I would have braced myself. I never cry when I am hurt usually. And the other thing was that Michael seemed quite changed. He is heavy and bony and rough, when he used to be gentle and careful. He doesn't seem to care how much he hurts me, although after the first time I didn't let him know that he does. So when I say that Lust is my besetting sin, I wonder really whether it is any more, and maybe it was only ever curiosity.

When I was little, I felt great pleasure. I remember sharing my bath with Michael, whose legs were longer than mine. His feet used to surface either side of my chest, and his little boy's thing bobbed in the water in front of my toes. I liked the look of his stronger arms and shoulders, and I know he liked to look at me. I would stay in the bath after he got out, and splash about a little, so he could watch me while he dried himself. He never said so, but I could tell he thought I was pretty. I would turn on my tummy and blow into the water, and then suddenly turn over again on to my back, to catch him looking at me. Sometimes he dried me from top to toe, very carefully, and then I would dry him again, in case he had missed any corners. We weren't at all shy, and Michael was never rough. I think if we wanted anything in those days it was to be like one another; we wanted to be both of us at once. But this was very difficult, so we started trying to take bits from one another by force. Then it seemed so unlikely to me that we would ever be allowed to share each other, that I worked out the plan of our marriage and the Will.

I don't think Michael has ever quite understood what I meant by our marriage. He has concentrated on the Assets and forgotten all about us. He made, for instance, a sickening fuss about his china frog, as if I cared who had it, now or at any time. But the latest subject to get in the way is Chemistry. All he thinks about now are his cleversticks experiments. Sometimes I wish he had never talked to grandfather. In the days when we first went to the laboratory – and after all, it was my idea to break into it – when it was our laboratory and not just Michael's, we used to talk to one another, or smoke together. Our wedding there was the happiest day in my life. I sat on the floor, sniffing at my flowers which I had borrowed from the vase in the morning-room, and listened to Michael reading that difficult story in his rather cautious voice (he talks as if he is asking questions all the time, so you never quite know whether he has finished or not), and I vowed to be good, and to do as he wished for ever. But now I think it was not the same for him; he saw that day as an end rather than a beginning, and ever since, as I said, I have had to recall him to our vows. Sometimes he even pretends not to notice when I spin my wedding ring at him.

It isn't really what I meant to happen, but it seems that things go wrong if you try too hard. When I try to be good, for instance, it is always disastrous. I am immediately worse than ever. I sometimes think I should try to be bad. Then perhaps there might be a chance that I would recoil in some sort of goodness.

When I still believed that my original plan could work, but saw how distracted Michael was, I decided it was time to proceed to the next step. I had fallen from the state of grace, and Michael looked old enough to me by last holidays – he looked at least as old as Mary's young man – so I decided we should try to have a baby. Michael pretended to be horrified at first, but I could tell he really wanted to agree. But now, since it's clear to me that the baby never even began – it was a false alarm, and Michael knows nothing about it one way or the other yet – I've had time to have second, and quite revolutionary thoughts. We must, I now think, instead of hanging on, give everything away, of our own free will: we could hold a sort of Free Church Fête in the summer holidays. But it means, too, that Michael and I must get some sort of Divorce. I didn't much like the sound of that when it first occurred to me, but now it seems inescapable, and I am going to suggest it to him at the beginning of the holidays.

The Prayer Book isn't much use when it comes to Divorce. I have been looking through it to see if there is a service that can help – a ceremony to unbind. There is only one that seems at all appropriate, and the more I read it the more I wonder at the futility of my original plan; how could I have imagined that we could hold on to anything, least of all to one another? We seem to be entailed beyond the reach of any Will or Testament. Well, I have realized this just in time. We have been 'of the earth, earthy' too long.

I don't know what Michael will think of this. I wish I could write to him, but he says other boys get hold of letters, and it's better not to risk it.

My friend Jane has been in a dreadful panic about these goings on. Her eyes nearly popped out of her head when I told her I thought I was having a baby. She simply didn't know what to think. It was quite convenient to let her do all the worrying for me: she asked all sorts of questions which it hadn't occurred to me to ask yet. When would the baby be born? where would I have it? what would I do with it? who would look after it? what would my parents say? would I be able to come back to school? how did I feel? was my tummy fatter yet? and so on. In fact I didn't feel any different, and perhaps that isn't surprising since it has turned out to be a false alarm. Apparently, I know this now, it's quite usual for the fall from the state of grace to be temporarily suspended for a few months at first.

It has been quite a hectic year. At the beginning of this term, Jane and I were confirmed, and that was another cause of concern for Jane. She has worried more about my immortal soul than her own. Would I confess all? How could I be confirmed if I hadn't? I think she expected me to go up in a puff of smoke when the Bishop laid his hands on me. In the end I reeled off a great list of things (my confession took much longer than anyone else's), particularly about how much food

I had stolen from the school larder, and how I read in bed after lights out, but everything I said seemed to bore the Clerical Codfish. It was clear he felt something worse lurked in my noxious depths.

'Have you not had any . . . er . . . um . . . impure thoughts, my child?' he asked, licking his lips.

'None, Father,' I answered. He likes to assume Catholic forms at these special moments.

'Nor committed any unclean deeds?'

Is it unclean to get married?

'No,' I replied.

So he reluctantly gave me absolution of my sins, and I was duly confirmed.

At the moment of my confirmation, I felt a great sense of nostalgia, though I'm not sure what it was for. The Bishop put his hand on my head and pressed it down very hard (I think I was trying to look up at him), so that my chin was jammed against my chest, and he kept his hand there long enough for me to begin to feel quite peaceful. I had shut my eyes and was just wishing he would leave his hand there for ever when he took it away, and my head, suddenly released, flew up on its stalk like a heavy seedpod that has been held down by a cat's paw.

And by the time I got back to my seat I knew I no longer believed in God.

I tested my new atheism on Miss X. I simply asked her, 'But who made God?' You would think I had thrown a bomb at her. She leapt up, strode to the centre of the classroom, turned round and round several times on the spot, and slowly came to rest pointing at me like a knife that is spun on the table, only I certainly wasn't the right answer.

'Fleur,' she thundered. 'God is.'

'Yes,' I said hopefully. '. . . is what?'

'Is. Is. God Is!' she shrieked. 'O fatal Pride!' and she turned that colour again.

I waited. She said no more. I'll never know from her what God is or isn't, or what he was before he wasn't, which is what I really asked.

Despite all this, I have still made room for Music. I wish sometimes I could like something less complicated, for Music too comes under Miss X's critical eye. She regards the choir with great suspicion in case we get carried away by the sound of our own voices, and anyone who practises too hard and long is told not to make so much noise. You can hardly avoid making a noise on these terrible pianos; I long for even the old piano in grandma's house. When I am playing, I forget what time it is, and I often sit on in the practice cell, without turning on the light, just to think. It is the next best thing to those lost early mornings. Sometimes I must admit I cry in there, although I couldn't really say why. Perhaps I may be missing Michael, but more often it is because I am fed up with this stupid school and Miss X and the Clerical Codfish.

I am learning a beautiful piece this term. It is called 'La Fille aux cheveux de lin' and it is by Debussy. The girl I imagine as I play it is about as different from me as I can possibly devise, and how I would like to be! – she reminds me I suppose of our head of school, who is thin and graceful and plays the cello. She is very vague and dreamy, and kind to the younger children when probably she should be ticking them off, and she has long wavy fair hair, of course. I imagine her sitting by a stream on a rather windy afternoon. It's important though not to get too 'carried away' by this picture, or the piece gets slower and slower, and once I stopped altogether just as the rather complicated bit, where you have to change your fingers on the same notes to keep it very smooth, begins at the top of the second page. 'Well, come back!' said my piano teacher. I like pieces that make pictures, and I think that the reason I don't much like Bach yet, although my teacher says I will when I'm older, is because I can't really see his music. I almost understood how I could get to enjoy it one day, though, when she played a 2-part invention to me recently, to see if I would like to learn it. It was so clever and neat and satisfactory. I felt as excited as I feel when I have understood a theorem. There's certainly no chance to stop during a piece like that; it was remorseless.

That is quite enough about school life for anyone's Memoirs, and I stopped writing there, at the end of term. Now I'm writing again, just after I've got home for the summer holidays. I've come straight to grandmother's, where we are staying, and before I even said hullo to Mary I rushed upstairs, flung off my school clothes, pulled on my shorts, and ran out into the garden. The first thing I always do is roll down the steep bank on to the lawn; I roll and bump and rub off the feel of school like a worn-out scabby snakeskin. Everything looks much the same, though perhaps it has shrunk a little. I pushed my way right round the woods (there are some strange sticks with numbers on them stuck in the ground at intervals), on round the laboratory (no sign of life there yet), and back through the kitchen garden where I picked a handful of raspberries. Then I sat and smoked under the oak tree for a while. I kicked off my sandals and my bare feet looked pleased to be back in the grass: they wriggled and pushed their way down through the old leaves and last year's acorns, and made themselves at home again.

So I didn't learn about Michael until I went round to see Mary in the kitchen. She told me he is not coming home for two more weeks; he's gone abroad on some school trip.

'Has he written to me?' I demanded, jumping down from the table ready to run and look in the hall.

'No, Miss Fleur,' said Mary, quite sternly for her. 'What would Master Michael be writing to you for? He's a busy boy.'

'To tell me, of course!' I cried. How could she be so annoying? For all Michael knew, he was due to be a father in six months' time, and he couldn't even bother to come home and find out. But I couldn't say that to Mary of course. I felt so angry and disappointed I couldn't stay with her (though I really like talking to her, and there was a lovely smell of rock cakes coming out of the oven). He is a deserter, a coward! When he comes home, I shall tell him we are having a baby, just to frighten him. I went up to his room, and stared at his school trunk which has just arrived, but there is no sign of the clutter that would be lying around if he was about to follow. I opened his window, and then suddenly burst into tears. I feel as if the holidays are ruined now, before they have even begun. It turns out he has gone climbing in Switzerland. Why does nobody tell me anything before it happens? Now I have been instructed not to sit under the oak tree any more; it seems as if it is too dangerous since that branch fell off last winter.

'What *can* I do?' I shouted at my father. I expected him to be angry, but he only said mildly that I should make the most of the rest of the garden, or help grandmother, who quickly gets tired these days as she works in her conservatory.

In the conservatory I calmed down. Grandmother too seems to have shrunk, and she is more like one of her water plants than ever (rather like the girl with the flaxen hair might become). This afternoon I have weeded all along one wall, and helped her with the watering. Even in summer the water from the well is icy cold. I hold on to the end of the long spout, and let the can gurgle down as far as it will go, then haul it up, half expecting to find it full of fish. Occasionally there is a frog, blue with cold, who looks astonished by the sunlight, and seems to grow greener by the minute as he dries under the leaves.

Mary brought us tea and the rock cakes (still warm!), and afterwards grandma and I played a game of Mah-Jong, although I have never known the rules very well, and she has almost forgotten them.

I think I will ask if I can sleep out in the garden at nights; that will be something different to do, until Michael comes home.

When I got home from Switzerland at the beginning of August, our parents announced almost at once that grandmother's house, the laboratory, and all the land were to be sold, although nothing would really be changed, since grandmother could stay on in the house as long as she liked, for the annual sum of a peppercorn. In fact, as the house was such a lot of work, and she did not really need all that room, she would use only the ground floor, and the flat upstairs could hold tenants, who would be very nice people and keep an eye on her. It would be an ideal arrangement. The woods had always been too dark, and they were to be cleared away, and the new estate that was to be built in their place would not come as close to the windows. The markers already stuck in the ground showed the boundaries. The oak tree would have to come down at once, but it had anyway become quite unsafe since its heaviest branch had fallen in last winter's storm. I think my parents had waited to break this news until I came home because they feared Fleur's reaction, and hoped that I would be a good influence on her. But Fleur sat stony-faced and silent throughout their explanations.

The next morning for the first time that holidays she spun her ring at me, but I pretended not to see, and avoided the laboratory for the first few days, although I was looking forward to getting back to my experiments. Eventually I went there, when I hoped she would not notice, but I had hardly begun to organize myself when Fleur climbed through the window.

'I'm busy,' I said. 'Can't you let me get on? I've got to work, not play, this holidays.'

Fleur narrowed her eyes.

'You are a coward,' she said. 'I didn't think you would desert me.'

'Desert nothing, stupid,' I said. 'It's all over. That game of the Will is finished. I never believed in it anyway. And what's more, we never got it signed, so even by your standards it is worthless.'

'It isn't finished,' said Fleur. 'It's just beginning. You began it, last holidays.'

'No,' I shouted. 'No, no, no.'

But Fleur just shrugged her shoulders, and said my shouting made no difference.

Our parents spent the summer sorting furniture, deciding what would stay with grandmother, labelling what could be sent to a local auction, what should go to London dealers, what to the tenants, what straight to their own house. The Louis Quinze desk and the rest of the French furniture was, it seemed, badly in need of restoration. Now too was the time to exchange the old piano for a better one; for several years it had been of little use to Fleur, who played less at home now grandfather was not there to enjoy her performances. Grandmother said little: she nodded in apparent agreement with the sensible suggestions as she sat by the unlit drawing-room fire facing grandfather's empty chair, or wandered around the conservatory with her long-spouted watering can.

My experiments were progressing well. I now had no trouble deciphering grandfather's system of annotation, and as he had said, all the relevant chemicals were on the shelves as he had left them, though some were in short supply. I used proportionately small quantities as I made preliminary exploratory measurements; my aim was to conclude the experiment that seemed the most unusual one by the end of the summer holidays. I spent nearly all my time in the laboratory, where I had rigged up a better light by connecting a gas pipe to an old light-fixture from the house. Fleur never came to see me after her first visit; if she was sent to find me for supper she stood outside and called to me, and had gone back to the house by the time I climbed out. By the first week in September, with only one more week to go, the last stage of the experiment was, I decided, ready to be conducted. Because I was a little worried about the result, which grandfather had not written up (or perhaps an exercise book was missing), I arranged for the final step to take place mechanically; I could observe its progress from a distance. The unconcluded notes seemed uncertain about the extent of the reaction, so in case I needed to make a quick getaway, I forced open the door which we had never used, but which was nearer to the workbench than the broken window.

I chose a day when I knew father would be back at work and Fleur was going to London with our mother to do some last-minute school shopping. If they left first thing, with luck they wouldn't be back until the evening, especially if Fleur's request to go to the cinema were granted. Everyone left on the early train as I had hoped, and by nine o'clock I was lighting up in the laboratory. I had never cleaned the windows for fear of drawing attention to my activities, so even though it was summer I relied on the improvised lamp. All morning I weighed and measured, increasing the quantities now by as much as the stores would allow, and brought the last phase to the point of readiness. At lunch time I returned to the house and raided the larder for a sandwich, which I ate with grandmother. I noticed that the Louis Quinze desk had already departed for the restorer. Then I lay in the sun on the rough grass by the stump of the oak tree and even fell asleep for a while.

By four o'clock I was ready. I shoved open the stiff unused door, re-lit the burners, and hung the weights that would enable the final additions to be tipped into position. 'Now!' I said, releasing the first weight. I ran to the door, and it was only when I got there that I remembered that I had meant to turn off the gas light. It wasn't important – the burners were still alight anyway – but I had thought it might be sensible. I looked anxiously through the doorway, but it was too late to go back. I blocked my ears and braced myself as the weights see-sawed meticulously and the phials swung slowly into position, just as I had planned.

The first drops were about to fall when I saw Fleur. She was climbing in the window at the back of the laboratory. 'Get out!' I screamed. She had one leg over the sill, and turned towards me in surprise. She grinned, and mischievously spun her ring at me in her old manner, swung her other leg up and over, and dropped down inside.

When the smoke had begun to clear, I crawled towards the laboratory, which seemed to have moved a long way off. Surely I had been standing just by it? I picked a path across the fallen bricks and charred pieces of wood for a while before I realized I was already inside what had once been the building. It was open to the sky. I couldn't tell where the door or the broken window had been.

Fleur lay on her back, and although her face was black with ash, she looked quite orderly, straight and still. I leant over her, and waited for her to open her eyes. But when she didn't, I began to study her carefully, as if I were reading her for the conclusion of my experiment. It seemed as if I had not looked at her for a long time, perhaps not since she was nine years old, when I had noticed how much paler and thinner she had grown, before I first took off my belt. Now she was more graceful, with small breasts, and slim arms. Her stomach under her summer frock was smooth and flat.

'Fleur,' I said, pleased. 'There is no baby. It's all right. You must have made a mistake.' I couldn't think why I hadn't questioned her more patiently. I took the curtain ring from her fourth finger and put it on my little finger, and spun it thoughtfully, before I turned to face the others, who were just beginning to arrive.

TWO

Unsolicited Gift

I never stood trial for the murder of my sister Fleur. My parents, numb with shock, asked me once what she could have been doing in the laboratory. I replied (at last they had asked): 'She was meeting me there' – but they seemed to lack the energy to pursue the enquiries I assumed must follow. At the inquest the blame was laid on my elders and betters, who had failed to disconnect the gas and dispose of the dangerous chemicals. My grandmother eventually moved, sooner than had been expected, into the Home, and we left the neighbourhood where perhaps we had never been fully welcome. The alien name disappeared from the local telephone book.

But all is not well with a boy who has a murder on his conscience. As I walked with my father away from the smoking ruins of the laboratory, I was disconcerted to find in myself a kind of irritation that I would not easily be able to establish what had gone wrong with my experiment. In the days that followed, at the funeral itself, as I laid on my sister's coffin a posy such as she had held at our wedding and whispered the words she would have approved – 'till death us do part' – even then one side of my mind was rechecking and counting, weighing and measuring, trying to identify the mistake I had made.

It is a mistake of another kind, one of sheer profligacy, to have lost at such an early stage the most lively and inventive character of one's acquaintance. A missing heroine is a structural disability. But as a result you could say that the rest of my life, and certainly the rest of this story, has been – will be – an attempt to replace her, to bring her back into the plot.

It was Fleur's absence, for instance, that led me to try to become a musician in her stead. That, and the stern eyes of the music student, our great-grandmother. And also, to some extent, a concern for the wasted new piano, for in the confusion of the funeral and removals it was quite forgotten to cancel the order for the instrument that was to replace the ancient Blüthner. The deposit had been paid; eventually the piano arrived; my parents had not the heart to put it in the drawing-room, and so it went into the spare room (the room that would have been Fleur's); and I started to play it. To my surprise, and to that of my family, I played very well. For good measure I took up the cello at the same time, and made 'exceptional progress', although it was always understood that I had begun 'too late'. In fact quite soon I had to all intents and purposes caught up with the others, and in a couple of years had learnt what it had taken them ten to master. At school the music and science departments laid siege to me, and battled for a stake in my future career, and from now on when I was working as a scientist I felt I should be practising, and when I was playing I missed the claims of science. Eventually, before I became a physicist (I took a First at Cambridge in 1959), I was for three years a would-be professional musician, studying first in London, and then in Paris.

I am reluctant to write about my life in Paris. What can I have done in Paris that every other English boy and girl – every other student – did not do? Occasionally I have read accounts by my peers of their time at, for instance, the Sorbonne and I have wearily, sometimes admiringly, ticked the items they are bound to display. Cafés: tick. Sex (French): tick, tick. Lectures (unattended) and demonstrations (usually missed): tick (gloomily), tick. Did I see Paris? Was Paris there while I was there? I think this is quite doubtful, as most of my time was spent on my own, either practising my cello in a small attic at the top of the house so as not to disturb other serious students, or lying in black despair on my bed. Black despair: tick. But sometimes I must have emerged for a music lesson, a rehearsal, or a concert, or even to buy a 'sandwich' and a demi-kilo of cherries. Everyone else seemed to be meeting people, and yet everyone was (you read now) lying on their beds in black despair: it is very curious. But I must have been there, and Paris must have been round the corner, since I can now return to look at the places where I was, officially, between October 1955 and June 1956. In fact I avoided and side-stepped every single sight and experience I was offered. If a fellow-student suggested I meet him for coffee, I said I had to practise; once or twice I came within a bottle's-length of a party, but I made sure I never knew the exact time, or lost the address. In cafés (I don't think anyone can entirely avoid cafés in Paris) I stuck my cello on the empty chair opposite me, and my head into a book. I turned up at the Louvre on Tuesdays, and at other galleries on Mondays: they were invariably shut. Except, that is, when I was taken in hand by a distinguished friend of my parents, who felt it was her role to civilize such an unfortunately ill-educated young Englishman. Together we stood patiently in front of the *Pietà d'Avignon*, waiting for my taste to develop. Development seemed always to mean either rapid progress in arrears, as far back in time as the Louvre could accommodate, or fast forwards to the present day, represented by the paintings in the flat of my elegant patroness, whereas my natural instincts seemed to hover without distinction somewhere in between. Occasionally I was summoned to lunch with her circle of young friends. Here then was my chance to meet my French contemporaries, but alas, the sophistication and glamour of this group – they were mostly drama students – reduced me to a state of Englishness bordering on the inane. Throughout lunch I struggled against violent indigestion: all my concentration was bent on controlling the currents of air that coursed up and down my system. The students of Jean-Louis Barrault did not wait for me to cap their quotations.

At anything more risky than a lunch invitation, such as the casual suggestion from one of the professors that I might like to move into a cheaper room in his house, I ducked violently and fled, in some inappropriate fear for my virtue. As a result I never went back to finish the course in harmony, and was not invited to play in a quartet, formed by the same professor from promising students within his reach, that went on to make quite a name for itself in Europe.

And so I missed, and missed out. I say I did not see anything, but rather I did not see what I saw. I saw Kiyoko Inoue. If an English girl spoke to me at the Conservatoire, I turned as cold as stone, and made sure she was convinced I was such a snob it would not be worth her while to try again. Anyway, I wished to speak French, not English (tick). Kiyoko Inoue said nothing at all, since both her English and French were almost non-existent. But when I, without thinking, smiled at her as she sat at the second desk of the first violins, she smiled back. Her mouth scarcely stirred, but I could tell that she smiled before her eyes returned quickly to the stand. In the break I took her a cup of coffee, and watched her smile from closer to.

Kiyoko Inoue and I had the purest relationship that has

ever intruded on the idea of Paris. I carried her music case; she lowered her eyes and seemed to smile. After a few weeks of this, she introduced me to salty seaweed titbits and real Japanese tea, which she made for me in her sitting-room (she was unusual in that she had two rooms), where I knelt on a mat specially laid out for the occasion. She knelt opposite me and poured the tea, and we alternately looked serious, sipped, and smiled. Sometimes, however, she tried to talk to me, but I did not help her out. 'Vous, you,' said Kiyoko Inoue bravely, extending her pale hand towards me, 'my frère, bro-ther, yes? I, sister? Votre amie, friend?' But I nibbled a piece of dried seaweed and frowned at her in feigned perplexity, until she lapsed, with a little sad smile, into silence.

Perhaps I was cruel to Kiyoko Inoue, who was as lonely as I? She was very beautiful. Before I departed from Paris, she had left the orchestra we both played in, and I heard that she was living with a Frenchman. I saw her once again in a café near the Conservatoire. She smiled at me frankly, and tutoyed me, which had not been our practice, but suddenly we both blushed and averted our eyes. I don't think Kiyoko Inoue could have gone back to Japan; her family would not have liked her to live with a Frenchman. It is surprising, come to think of it, that she was allowed to study music abroad, or at least, to live on her own. Five years later, on my way to take up my research in Heidelberg, I tried to find out if she was still in Paris. The Conservatoire and the Japanese Embassy helped me in my search for a while, but she had vanished without trace. Probably her name had changed by then.

By the time Kiyoko Inoue was living with a Frenchman, I was in fact involved with a French girl. Perhaps my preamble wasn't as accurate as it might have been, but these facts shouldn't detract from the general truth of what I said. For my statutory affair with a French girl was absolutely irrelevant. It is hard for me to say it, but Germaine was deadly, not pretty, not clever, not intelligent, not musical, not anything, really, except French, and that was obligatory. (I don't know any more whether this deserves a tick or not.) 'My French girlfriend' was a Communist, which at first I thought would be modernizing, but it turned out to mean that we could have no debate. If I asked her, politely and admittedly indifferently, what she had been doing, whom she had seen, she replied 'C'est confidentiel!' It was mortifying, and I soon stopped enquiring. Germaine was the sort of Communist who puts hygiene before even practical romance. For her, weekly sex was part of a healthy régime, like emptying the bowels or going to the gymnasium. She was always in such a hurry, probably to get to a meeting of her cell, that she never even took off all her clothes. Our confrontations were painfully impeded by the presence of unwieldy garments that did more than anything to dispel for me the Myth of Paris.

For that is what it was, and for all I know, still is: a Myth. After all these years, I am left with no more than a few clichés, fewer ticks, and a shudder at the thought of Germaine's crooked teeth (oh, I had not mentioned those?).

I have reluctantly considered that account; it makes pretty depressing reading. Was everything really so shifty, shifting, shiftless, hopelessly misunderstood? Didn't a single thing happen that led anywhere, if only inwards? I suggested, I see, that Kiyoko Inoue was lonely. Perhaps the one experience that Paris imparted unequivocally to the flotsam and jetsam of students on her mythical streets was that of loneliness, a loneliness that was the worse for being completely inadmissible. When, nowadays, I occasionally feel again that awful sense of drift, as if you have suddenly been cut loose, marked (in invisible ink) 'Lost, Stolen, or Strayed', I can only say that it reminds me at once of Paris. Late autumn evenings, the smell of burning leaves, grinding traffic, and lamplight on the crowded hustling streets; that loosening at the pit of the stomach: c'est Paree. But I could go on like this indefinitely: these are the hollow grins of loneliness. Perhaps the nearest I got to describing it was when I referred to Kiyoko Inoue's little sad smile as I pretended not to understand what she was trying to say to me. Yes, I should have stopped there.

And now another problem has cropped up. Not only have I lost my original heroine, but now I wonder if it is the same narrator telling this story; that is, am I the same as I was then, at the beginning, and as I suddenly glimpsed I am going to be in, say, eight years' time if ever I get round to that part of the story? Obviously not, in some ways, and yet I'm bound to make the connections, to 'establish the character', if you like, so that I at least can believe that the boy who blew up the laboratory and in so doing killed his sister, also knelt as a music student in front of Kiyoko Inoue and slept with an ugly French girl, and will, by the time this ends, have done as a man goodness knows what else. My glimpse just now was of someone rather urbane and reserved standing at what looked like a University party, but could have been the Max Planck Institut's annual get-together. Before I get time to look round (am I married currently, for instance?) – the door opens, and in comes, on the arm of a Frenchman (husband, ami, friend?) – But stop! Let's get back to the present, that is, to where this story is at present. It is too soon to turn it into a romantic novel. And yet I realize I have firmly decided – perhaps at that very moment, just as the door opened and I was about to shut my eyes, wondering if I would ever dare open them again – to try for a happy ending.

Can you better what is done? The explosion and the fate of my young sister upset people; they were genuinely disturbed by the violent and unhappy outcome. Don't think I haven't asked myself, was it really necessary? Did she have to die? She could have jumped up briskly and . . . But after a certain point it isn't as simple as that; these things won't exactly unwrite themselves. Miscible ingredients don't separate themselves out again. Still, I have resolved to see if I can't make sure of a happier ending, in the end.

But where am I now? Already about to leave Paris. I am afraid I have fallen into the familiar trap of identifying places by the women I met in them. I was, let me remind myself, in Paris for the sake of music, for my lessons with a celebrated French cellist and at the same time a little experience in the student orchestra and any chamber music I had the energy to attach myself to. The Quartet was launched and did perfectly well without me; but I was involved in the formation of an early music group. Although the revival of interest in early music had continued and developed since the War, it was not until a few years later that it was to come to the forefront of musical fashion. It was still just possible for us not to feel too uncomfortable, for instance, that we were playing on modern instruments, though we made the concession of holding our bows in the manner of viols, palm upwards. The group consisted of five string players and two singers, soprano and countertenor, and we gave several concerts in ill-lit and empty Parisian churches. Our high spot was a date for a provincial Festival, which was inaccurately and lavishly reviewed as only the French provinces can review: 'ces jeunes musiciens charmants, fils du vingtième siècle et en outre de notre Conservatoire, nous ont transportés au Moyen Age, âge des troubadours, du poète Villon' et cetera. It predicted for us a place among the immortals, but we had already decided to make our way there by separate routes. I for instance had been for a few months committed to a frantic correspondence with my parents and various universities, and was now to resume my scientific studies where I had left off, taking up an earlier offer of a place at Cambridge.

Shakespeare had access to and, heavens knows, had earned the right to certain conventions that saved him a lot of trouble. Imagine if, in *The Winter's Tale*, he had had to cover explicitly the sixteen-year gap in the story. He knew his audience didn't want to hear about Paulina's comings and goings with trays and jigsaws; nor to see how sweetly pretty were Perdita's first tottering steps. They weren't interested in the effect on rustic vocabulary of the absence of primary education in the Bohemian countryside; nor even, much, in the annual culling of bears that had become such a gruesome necessity. Simply one day, after everyone has had time to grow up or grow old, a falcon flies off course; a young man runs in, probably in rather a bad temper (his friends are doing better with more experienced birds), and – hey presto – it is Love at First Sight between the Prince and the Shepherd's Daughter (only of course, she isn't), and it is clear by the time we turn up after the interval that everything will be all right. *And it is.*

But I suppose I can't employ the Chorus to take up this tedious time for me, though perhaps Autolycus might scatter a few red herrings at a price . . .

Such is my perversity, that as soon as I was safely ensconced in the Cambridge laboratories, all my spare attention and time was spent on remaining a musician. I can hardly remember going to sleep during my university years, as I led a double life which, after a day at work in the laboratory, followed by an evening's rehearsal or concert, would resume at night in the laboratory. I think the two worlds I moved in had little inkling of one another; if I 'went missing' from one, it was not at a crucial moment: music could be fitted in between 5 and 11 p.m.; physics from 11 p.m. until dawn, and of course in the daytime. I had breakfast with scientists, supper with musicians – and no purely personal friendships: there would not have been time for them. If in later years I met someone who had been up at Cambridge with me, he would say, 'oh yes, the physicist' or 'oh yes, the musican', and I would know at once in which context we had met.

In my final year a professional tenor asked me to play in a series of university concerts he was giving with his recently founded early music Consort. As I took off my white overall and picked up my instrument, I didn't stop to ask myself whether the two activities were inimical to one another. Surely, you might assume naively, you were happier playing the lute or gamba (for by now I had moved on to contemporary instruments) than pursuing the destructive abstractions of your grandfather's career? It did not present itself like that, and certainly not as a choice between forms of happiness. I could not tell you even now whether the laws of physics and of music are in opposition, or profoundly necessary to one another, but I suspect it would be a simplistic view that set them in deadly conflict, as if they represented head against heart, reason against emotion, Apollo versus Dionysus. It would be too easy, at a more personal level, to say that while the pursuit of science, since that first explosion, has proved catastrophic to me, music has on the contrary lured me back to humanity, to the best relationships in my life, to my better self. I would resist this interpretation of events and search rather for their interdependence.

In the early days this perambulation between science and music had, if I cared to exploit it, all the advantages of irresponsibility. Like a man with a substantial private income, I did not feel obliged to make stringent selections: the way up could be contemplated while I took the way round. But I was lucky enough to fall on my feet in both lives. I marked out the lines of my research at Cambridge, and was later able to resume work at the Max Planck Institut, and in between I joined the tenor and for two years worked with the Consort.

It occurred to me to omit at this point a dismal sequence of events. An author preparing his Collected Works late in life may surely be free to exclude anything that is irrelevant or badly done, or that he now judges embarrassing or meaningless in his *oeuvre*. To whom does he owe a complete explanation? In my case, I am referring, of course, to my first marriage, and if I do recount the basic facts it is partly for the very reason that it will not fit neatly into the category of 'Science: Distressing Experiences' and 'Music: Vice Versa'. For my first wife, while not symbolizing either Science or Music, was a musician, and our marriage lasted only six months before she moved over, or back really, to the tenor. I think now that I only married her because she loved the tenor (he took longer to decide about her, but my intervention helped him to make up his mind). I always knew she was in love with him; she talked about him incessantly, and at first I merely comforted her when their affair had apparently foundered. Under the guise of sympathetic listener I graduated, still listening, into her bed, while she heard only, in the distance, the voice of the tenor. The Consort was on tour in Manchester when my wife came back to our hotel room and suggested she move along the corridor; and certainly it seemed much more convenient. The curious thing is that I helped her pack; I made none of the gestures I imagined it would be appropriate to make. If anything I felt quite sympathetic. I didn't exactly congratulate the tenor (in fact I did not speak to him much from then on), but you would be wrong if you thought I was nursing a desire to hit or to poison him. I waited until the end of the tour, and then departed.

But it would be cheating to suggest that matters really ended there. For what about the tenor? He held us all in the palm of his hand, or rather, in the coil of his throat. Like fascinated snakes we waved our heads and played for him when he sang. Even writing this, I am shocked to find myself shaking with nervousness – is it anger? or fear? – but what have I got to be angry about or afraid of? He retrieved my mistake, for which I can only thank him. And for two years we made music, enchanter and enchanted, drawn as the celebrated analogy has it, like impotent moths into his flame.

And so, about seven years after I left Paris, I am to be found at the Max Planck Institut for Nuclear Physics in Heidelberg. You will remember that on my way there two years previously, I had called on a half-formulated impulse at the Japanese Embassy in Paris, in a vain attempt to track down Kiyoko's present whereabouts.

How hard it is to record the details of years that have meant so little, and in retrospect seem to have consisted largely of absence. Those years in Heidelberg (but your work? the quartets you played in the evenings?) are reduced in my mind to no more than a series of long walks through the silver birch woods around the Institut. Half my waking life, more, has been passed in limbo, and if you add to that the hours one spends asleep (but in my case these are comparatively few) you could work out I have only been 'alive' about five years of my fifty so far. Oh, I have functioned in the other forty-five, and effectively by worldly standards, but only intermittently have I felt that fusion of thought and emotion in myself, the understanding, that I would grace with the name of living, that makes life 'worth' living. A woman might nod complacently and say 'oh, you must mean when you have been in love' – but no, Fräulein, that would be to assume too much. Those moments have had to do with both physics and music, and that again encourages me in my instinctive view that the two disciplines are not essentially at odds. The exaltation of understanding may occur in either field; for it is not, finally, a sense of mystery that excites me. I am not, that is, titillated in a vague, semi-mystical way by music, but when I best understand how it is working. I see that I ask 'how' and not 'to what end?' In the theatre too, nothing pleases me more than to see the workings backstage, to catch sight of an actor 'hidden' for a moment in the wings, blowing his nose, or a dancer rubbing his calf muscles before he assumes the expression and pose of his role and steps boldly forth. Illusion is not interesting in itself, only in how it is achieved.

Sidestepping still the question as to whether the end of a series of chords is not the same as that of an exposé of physical laws, I would venture that in myself both may produce an identical tension and, in moments of mastery, that rare orgasm of mind that makes it impossible to distinguish emotion from mental vigour. Nor is this as hedonistic in intent as it may sound, for nothing could be more certain than that to search for this pleasure as an end in itself would be fatal and perverse. If that were to happen, the work would be compromised; the figures faked, the notes hurried over and flattered in a too easy search for glib resolution. But I see I may be confusing myself; all I am really saying is that I respond with the same mixture of mind and emotion, regardless of the matter in hand. This isn't to say very much about the nature of physics and music themselves.

As I walked alone through the woods above the Institut each afternoon (to stay in the canteen after lunch was to become embroiled in local politics and in-fighting), I was alive in a way that I was not the rest of the time. Tenuous suggestions flickered through my mind like the intermittent sunlight falling between the branches on to my face; the birds sang as if to encourage – or could they teach? – me from the high tips of the trees. Much of my original work was done on these walks, that is, clues and connections came to me as if my regular stride insisted on the advancement of thought. Sometimes I would find myself, quite late in the afternoon, running down the last metres to the Institut in my hurry to get back to the laboratory. Those were my best days. They were not to be contrived or sought, although I came to think as I grew older that they had a rhythm of their own that one could learn to accommodate; it was perhaps basically seasonal. I have never done any good work in the hot summer months, for instance, and between late September and about April am at my most active. The most you could hope to do in the in-between times was to hold yourself in a state of readiness, though God knows what this entailed. There was work to be done, then, that undone would waste precious time when the more creative moments struck. You had to go doggedly on, pushing through uncut undergrowth, to be able to break cover and run down the last slope.

So perhaps I was wrong, or romantic, after all, to suggest that I am only 'alive' on those final runs, when the sensation of pleasure is predominant. It is simply that it is hard to focus on the man as he hacks and shoves through the dark dull periods of unproductive work or worse, of waiting to be able to work. At those times he has no sense of himself, except as obdurate and ungiving material, and is aware only of the intractable unrelatedness of things. A 'state of readiness' for a physicist or a musician is to have been working without pleasure and perhaps without a sense of direction, indefinitely. And to return to the Fräulein whom I rebuffed just now: in matters of love (and possibly in religious belief), if she will consent to mere analogy, the necessary precondition must be a fine mixture of readiness and passivity. It occurred to me to say 'emptiness'. (The Fräulein, who is of a mystical disposition, scenting ecstasy, moves in on my passivity and encounters unexpected resistance.)

My three years at Heidelberg then could all be summed up in the afternoon I crashed out of the woods like a wild boar and leapt over the ditch in my haste to get back to the laboratory. I fell over and twisted my ankle, and when I eventually hobbled in, swearing in a variety of tongues that impressed the research assistants, could not for the life of me remember what I had deduced.

But now I am in a hurry to get back to that party I began to tell you about. The party was at the University, where a European quartet of some repute was being entertained: it was the quartet I had seen forming when I was a student in Paris. I had surprised myself this week by going backstage after one of their concerts to greet the cellist (whose lessons had followed mine in those days). So here I was at this party, representing a mixture of interests: the British, the Musical Connection, and a salutary breath of Establishment Science. I was not representing anything for the moment, however, but simply standing on the edge of the gathering refilling my pipe, when the heavy door opened again. I don't know, I shall never know, what came over me: I was suddenly filled with a sense of hope so sharp that I had to shut my eyes to contain it, and once they were shut I couldn't bring myself to open them again. Why now? Perhaps the nostalgia and slight upheaval of seeing these musicians, half acquaintances, from an unpursued life of the past, an alternative life, had unsettled me. Perhaps, after all, those missing years and more have to be accounted for. Ridiculous really. But one can't stand indefinitely at a University party with one's eyes shut as an indefinable sense of hope floods through one's limbs, so with a dreadful effort, more afraid than I had ever felt in my life, I dragged my eyes open and looked back at the door. Hardly a moment can have passed; the door was still opening, and in came, on the arm of a Frenchman, my sister, amie, friend. It was Kiyoko Inoue. You will realize what a state I was in when I tell you that I nearly said, It was Fleur. No. It was Kiyoko Inoue, or whatever her name was by now. Something was the matter with me at this party. I dropped my pipe and trod on it, breaking the stem, and my hand was shaking as I took another gulp of my drink. I didn't of course look round to see if I was married: I knew quite well I no longer was.

The Cultural Attaché from the British Embassy introduced me to Mlle Kiyoko Inoue that evening.

'But that is not your name,' I said foolishly, as I held her pale hand.

'It is, again,' she said calmly.

'Then we are quits,' I said, and that is all that was said on the subject of the exchange of names.

I have found as I write this account, which is too full of feelings, both absent and present, that repeatedly I have only clichés to ape them. There seems to be nothing new to say: in this field, what has been done can hardly be bettered. I must rely on your knowing what I mean when I say that it was as if we had just arrived back in Kiyoko's rooms with her music case, and I at last answered the tentative remarks she had made to me eight years before. And though I am having this problem of finding the right language for the story, the language problem was no longer one for us as we chattered and laughed. Of course it never had been really. Kiyoko, who had continued to live in Paris after I had left, now spoke quite elegant French and her English was very far from inadequate.

It was only recently that she had moved to Germany so my German was better than hers, but I had no doubt that if she remained she would soon catch up.

Is this, then, so soon, the happy ending I told you I would try to find? Would Kiyoko Inoue stay around until the end? But nothing is as straightforward as that, and after only a few weeks things went strangely wrong. I mentioned that, in my confusion at the party, I had nearly said 'it was Fleur'. This confusion began to overtake me again, and eventually to possess me, so that when I opened my mouth to say 'Kiyoko' the name of Fleur rushed to my lips. Soon it was as much as I could do to keep my mouth shut and be silent, as her name insisted in my head. Deafening silences filled the spaces which I longed to fill with Kiyoko, and after a while Kiyoko grew quieter too. When we made love, Kiyoko's face and Fleur's, woman's and child's, merged on the pillow before me until all I dared do was grit my teeth against her neck and pray that I did not shout my sister's name out loud. At last, one night, I knew I could stop myself no longer. I was so terrified that I jumped out of bed and left the house. I walked round the town all night until the din subsided; and then I went back to where Kiyoko lived. Nothing was mentioned then, but that evening, as we were sitting in a bar,

'Who is Fleur?' said Kiyoko Inoue.

I looked at her and didn't reply. It seemed to me she knew already.

'You talk about her in your sleep, you know,' she said.

'She was my sister,' I replied.

Kiyoko's expression didn't change. 'Will you tell me what happened?' she asked. 'How did you come to kill her?'

So I told her. I think I hoped that Kiyoko Inoue would just go away now and not ask any more questions. But she sat on beside me with her hand on top of mine. Our hands lay there without moving for a long time.

She came home with me that evening, and then, I really don't know how to go on with this, but all hell was let loose. Sometimes people suggest that by talking or writing you can change things, as if your real life, or somebody's real death, could be transformed by a few well-chosen words, however symbolic or schematic. If anything, the opposite had happened.

'I am not Fleur,' said Kiyoko Inoue throughout that night. What else could she say? The next morning I began to cry, and I cried for twenty-four hours without stopping.

The progress of my crying was as follows:

At first it was as if an iron hand had seized my stomach, and was wringing it and twisting it. I retched and moaned, and was as sick as a dog. Kiyoko came and went, occasionally reorganizing the bed, or changing the bowl by my side. Later in the day, I lay and shivered. I was so cold I rattled like dry leaves scuttling across a draughty street. During this time, Kiyoko got into bed beside me and tried to keep me warm. That night I began to weep; I wept as if I were a sluice for everything that could flow through me and out of me, as if I were draining away. As I wept, Kiyoko continued to come and go beside me; several times perhaps she replaced my sodden pillow, or pushed back the soaking hair from my forehead. When I stopped crying abruptly – one moment I was crying, the next I was not – she arrived almost at once with a mug of something very hot and very delicious. This was the morning of the next day. I fell asleep instantly.

THREE

Freelance Rates

There is a crucial difference between the enjoyment of playing for its own sake and the exhilaration of public performance. My main problem as a professional musician had been that I did not enjoy performing. As a cellist in Heidelberg, in a good amateur quartet, I was at ease: we played (we might stop, experiment, play again) – but we did not have to go through those agonizing preconditions of performance, which reduced my nails to shreds, caused my pulse to race, and my hands to sweat, symptoms which persisted on the concert platform, whereas my fellow musicians were it seemed transformed as they stepped on to the stage into creatures of unbounded confidence, who radiated a capacity for display. I played very well – don't misunderstand me. The tenor would not have engaged me if I had not. But except on rare occasions, usually the more informal ones, or in rehearsal when I could relax enough to relish the others' performance, and indeed, the music, I didn't enjoy myself. Partly I blame my lack of pleasure on the fact that as a child I never acquired the habit of performance. Fleur played regularly to an admiring audience of relations, and at school had already won piano competitions and performed in concerts. When she sat down at the piano it was as if her impatience and scornfulness (always otherwise to the fore) were tossed aside with her plaits. She was a performer, perhaps, even before she was a musician. Her understanding of how music worked was, I think (though it is difficult to reconstruct her talent in retrospect) largely emotional. She played best from memory, which left her free to wield her audience, and she would be entirely thrown if she lost her place: she could not work herself back harmonically. Maybe this sort of talent, based on instinct, the sensation of sound, and a sense of power, could not have survived unchanged into her adult life.

It was left to me to develop a more articulate kind of musicianship. My performing sense has always been subordinate to a sort of argumentativeness, or persuasiveness, on the part of the music itself. I have an unromantic view of the performer's role; sometimes I even felt a great temptation to stop and break the spell (the spellbinder on whom our performances depended when I was a professional was, of course, the tenor). I did not believe in holding an audience in the palm of my hand. Such ambivalence in a performer, a sort of perverse renunciation of power – as if the Pied Piper had left the rats wondering whether or not to jump into the River Weser – creates an aura of detachment around music which many people find disconcerting. The warm murmur of approval that would follow the performance of one such as Fleur – or the tenor – is in my case replaced by a faint rustle of, one might almost say, dissatisfaction. Is there not more than that, it seems to wonder? Are we still here? Is it over? . . .

Kiyoko, who argued with me about this in Heidelberg, insisted that I was greatly overstating the case. She said that from my account no one could possibly imagine I could play at all, let alone make anyone want to listen, and what about my recordings of the Bach gamba sonatas, which had sold so well in recent years? Maybe, then, all I am talking about is, once again, my own sense of myself as a performer, for the music seems to have made its own way despite my scruples.

Examine, then, the musician in action. First of all he is, precisely, in action. Normally I am rather still: I sit quietly and watch people. But when I play I become extremely active. I have to heave my cello or gamba out of its case, rub rosin on the bow, find the chair that has once again got into the wrong room, adjust the music stand that Kiyoko last used. And then there is the playing: my right arm flies madly backwards and forwards, bucketing and curvetting; my left hand scuds furiously up and down the fingerboard; even my head, that normally inclines broodingly over a pipe, whips from side to side. It is rather like the strange and sudden transformation of two people who one moment were lying quietly side by side in bed and now break into the dash and clutch of passion. I am used to listening, but now a quite new sort of attention is demanded. The ears do not 'pick up' sound so much as depend on it; they are plugged in to the source itself. That day I played the Bach *Sonata no. 2 in D Major* and tried deliberately to detect the moment when sound takes over from my manufacture of it. But by the Allegro I had begun to work so hard that I forgot what I was looking for, and it was only when I came to a flourishing halt and threw back my head to see Kiyoko leaning against the door listening that I realized the music had won again. We both burst out laughing.

'It is the Allegro', she said, 'that is irresistible. Even without the harpsichord.' (And I remembered an occasion when, hearing the tenor begin to sing at an orchestral rehearsal, I had simply dropped the newspaper I was reading offstage and moved as if mesmerized into the hall to listen to him.)

'But if I played it like this?' I said: I played a passage unrhythmically and using too much bow.

'I would not love it, or you,' said Kiyoko, putting her hands to her ears and smiling at me through her fingers. It is she that is irresistible! I played the passage once more to set such a serious matter to rights. Then my experiments were postponed until another evening.

Despite all I have said about my dislike of performing, I agreed while we were still in Germany to give a lute recital for a cultural event arranged by the Institut. Perhaps the temptation to combine my lives was too great. I at once regretted accepting, as all the old symptoms of stage-fright seeped back. Kiyoko was concerned, but I could tell that even she was surprised at the extent of my nervousness. She drove me to the hall and stood for a while helplessly in the green room as I paced up and down, biting my nails, and smiling at her vacantly as if she were a stranger. Through the fog of horror, I could just sense her dismay.

'Go and get yourself a seat, where I can see you,' I begged her. She went slowly away, as reluctantly as if she were leaving me to undergo a major operation. I glimpsed her pale face in about the sixth row when I came on to the platform, and then, as my slithery hand clutched at the lute, my head cleared: I woke up. Kiyoko was there; I would play for her.

I moved my chair and footstool nearer to the front of the stage, tuned at leisure, smiled at Kiyoko, and began to play, out of my planned sequence, a piece of which she was particularly fond. I was aware, distinctly, of the audience's puzzlement; a few pages were flipped backwards and forwards as people searched their programmes in an attempt to work out what I was doing, but I ignored this and deliberately, as it were, played them down. While part of me, memory and fingers, performed, another part, will and eyes, remained quite separate and for the first few minutes strayed over the audience as if I were raking it in to my feet. The pages stopped turning; a stillness fell; I moved closer – that is, I drew the audience closer – and played now to Kiyoko, and saw her relax. Then I turned from the audience and from Kiyoko, back to the lute itself and played, eyes bent on the instrument, my ears pinned to the sound that tumbled through my hands. It was a long piece, one I usually left to the second half of a programme, but the audience did not stir. As I stood up at the end I could see Kiyoko's hands holding her cheeks: she was not crying? But no, she was smiling and clapping now, with the rest.

'We are on, Fleur!' I said to myself, to the performer in myself. I have never played so well! Or should I say, I have never enjoyed myself so much?

'It is all for you, I was playing for you,' I told Kiyoko later that night. But Kiyoko is wiser. 'Oh no,' she says. 'But I am glad I am here. How solemn you looked when you came on to the platform. I thought you had forgotten how to smile. Look at me! In future you must practise smiling, not scales.'

We laugh so much we almost forget how to make love.

Better far, then, to play after all. And at the end of that year we moved to London, where I was surprisingly quickly back in the swim on a freelance basis. Kiyoko was pregnant already; we had decided to have a child, perhaps two, as soon as possible.

For our wedding present, my parents gave Kiyoko the Louis Quinze desk.

I wish I could paint for you the picture of Kiyoko seated at the desk where I had so often seen my grandmother busying about her domestic arrangements. I had not wanted this desk: it had been a point of honour with me never to receive it. But I could not help but see it might have been designed for Kiyoko. Her slim legs folded neatly under it; her small hands flew in and out of the pigeon holes and little drawers as she excitedly explored it; even her shiny black hair matched the beautifully tended lacquered surfaces.

'You can't type on it?' I said to her dubiously.

'What does that matter?' she cried. 'It is simply lovely! Oh, thank you, thank you!' Her enthusiasm caused both my parents to blush with the pleasure they attempted uselessly to conceal at the success of their gift.

And so the Louis Quinze desk did indeed arrive at our flat, and found its new place in Kiyoko's room. (Her typewriter remained on the kitchen table.) She now spent most of her days experimenting with translating Japanese children's stories, and the evenings preparing a tempting nursery for the child. I would come home late after a concert and find her perched, her stomach curved like a bow, on the top of the ladder, conscientiously painting a frieze of Japanese fairy-tale creatures round the wall.

'Those bears look pretty frightening to me,' I commented. Kiyoko regarded me quite scornfully. 'You must remember that this is to be a half Japanese baby,' she said. 'How did the concert go?'

'So, so. *Don't jump!*' But she jumped lightly down on top of me, and she was to remain very active and agile until the last few weeks of her pregnancy. Kiyoko was longing for the arrival of the child which she was convinced would be a boy (who would not fear the bears on the wall); I was a little less sure, and indeed found it very hard to visualize the prospective person.

'But how do you know it will be a boy?' I would enquire cautiously.

'I want it to be one, that looks just like you.'

'Poor boy. But it might be, just might be, a girl, that looks just like you?' And so on. But these exchanges, growing increasingly more meaningful as the bow of Kiyoko's body was drawn tighter, eventually got through to me. A girl? I secretly decided I would prefer a daughter, first at least. So long as Kiyoko didn't mind too much.

If I had become a father a few years earlier, maybe I would not have been present at the birth of the child, but by this time it seemed to be quite a matter of course that I should, or at least, could be there. Had I ever imagined such an event in the past, it would have taken place in the context of a nineteenth-century novel, in which the male traditionally paces up and down, beating his brow and vowing (after a night of infidelity) to reform his life utterly, if only everything will go well. But here I was, dressed in a professional white gown and with a mask over my mouth, through which I tried to reassure Kiyoko when she turned her beleaguered face back to me.

These days you are told so much and people talk so freely about their experience of birth that you should know what to expect. You go into it, perhaps quite dangerously, feeling you do indeed know what to expect. But nothing, not all the information, statistics, and exercises, can explain away in advance the violence and remorselessness of what seemed to us to be an extraordinarily long drawn-out birth. (I have been sure ever since that death, if it is not instantaneous, will be a similarly uncontainable experience.) For about a week afterwards I could not hold my bow properly, so tightly had Kiyoko clung to my hand. I mention that: it is only the merest selfish detail. It is not easy to watch someone else doing all the work, and such hard and dreadful work. I wanted to shout at the doctor and nurses to stop it at once at all costs; it wasn't possible that Kiyoko should have to try any longer. But Kiyoko, as she came back to earth between contractions, and her familiar and calm voice reasserted itself, said each time 'Please don't go, you're far too useful'. I don't know who was reassuring whom. I mopped her dishevelled forehead; she gripped my hand; and the struggle resumed, until at last our daughter was born.

My daughter was born a few days after my own birthday, on 11 March 1965. I think my first feeling towards her was almost one of anger, in that she had hurt Kiyoko so much. Then, as I peered at her, I felt sure I had seen her before somewhere, although it wasn't at all clear what she really looked like as she waved her fists in front of her wrinkled red face and yelled without stopping for the first hour of her life.

'Oh, a girl! All right,' said Kiyoko.

'She looks quite fierce enough to stand up to the bears,' I said. I couldn't bring myself to let go of Kiyoko's hand by now. After a while, despite the yells of the baby, she suddenly fell asleep, looking very exhausted but contented, and even pleased with herself. We were left alone, with the baby lying in the crook of her arm, and eventually it stopped crying and fell asleep too. I gazed at it anxiously: was its heart still beating? Say it rolled off the bed? How could two creatures that looked so perilously fragile have proved themselves to be so strong? I leant over them to catch their mingled breathing: Kiyoko's steady and slow, and smelling sweet, the baby's quick and snuffly, and faintly, though not disagreeably, sour. I felt entirely inadequate to look after them: I had even, I found, begun to tremble in the way I associated usually with a form of nervous sexual excitement. I sat back and kept my eyes riveted on them, though by now I too was so tired I could hardly keep awake, until at last I was released from my post by a couple of nurses, who had come to wheel them away to their own room.

I have not been able to decide whether it is too difficult for a man to observe his own sex in action, and therefore whether the picture I present is too diffident to be convincing. But after the birth of my daughter I became increasingly aware of myself by contrast to her. A man who can hold a tiny child in one hand, at least during the first few weeks of its life, is forced to come to terms with the fact of his formidable power over a defenceless creature, and since it is at once clear to him that he may never wield that power (at least, not intentionally) he simultaneously releases a source of gentleness in himself that he may never otherwise have tapped. While Kiyoko and the infant had seemed so fragile, but proved themselves at the birth itself and now daily to be so strong, I appeared, by reason of my size and function, powerful, and yet became in practice daily more scrupulous through my dealings with the child. Kiyoko was far more carefree and matter-of-fact in her handling of it. I would wince when, for instance, she briskly dumped it down on the tabletop to change its nappy (admittedly it didn't seem to mind, but only waggled its legs the more gaily). When I changed it, I felt as if I were dealing with a transplanted shoot that would bruise or break at the slightest mishandling. My fingers were used to delicate work; they were automatically well-controlled. But never had they felt so acutely aware of both their power to damage and their capacity to be gentle as when they bathed, or dried, or changed my daughter.

She was, though, as robust a baby as you could wish for, sturdy and pink-cheeked, and on the whole more European-looking than Japanese at this stage, except for her distinctly slanted eyes and signs of fine jet-black hair. I said that the moment she was born I had felt I recognized her, and it didn't take me long to see how much like my sister she looked – at least, my sister as I first remembered her when she was a baby and I, a boy of three, had stared at her in her crib. Perhaps I said this more times than was tactful, for Kiyoko appeared unusually defensive, and would quickly point out the baby's more Japanese features. Anyway, we agreed to call her Sumi, which seemed to resolve the matter.

A man is at his most interesting not when he is in his traditional posture in the prime of his life, aggressive, powerful, and dominating, but rather, I came to think, as he learns to subdue these capacities in a play of a more tentative nature. But I did not express this so clearly to myself at the time as, by contrast, from day to day, I acted the necessary (and painful) role of assertive breadwinner.

If this is what a father may feel towards his baby daughter, what can such a little creature make of this figure who is her father? The mother is another matter: someone to be plundered, resorted to, blamed and rewarded in an entirely savage interchange of necessity. But this huge and half-unfamiliar visitant: what of him? How strangely delightful are his attentions from the very earliest days, made all the more so by the apparent perilousness of his presence, granted and removed, it seems, beyond any power of hers to choose. While a little girl may see the need to mollify her mother, it will be in a relationship that is (at least in those early uncivilized days) based on a bargain; her father, on the other hand, she, out of wanton pleasure, seeks only to please. Kiyoko, observing Sumi chuckling at me as I tucked her up one night said, with a mixture of jealousy and admiration,

'She loves you already far more than she will ever love me! What a hussy she is!'

'Oh come!' I said, half-embarrassed, half self-deprecating, but I was a hypocrite, for I knew it already to be true. And in this too I saw the case for a sort of abnegation of power; I could not properly cultivate my daughter's unconditional offer of love. Is it from this necessary reticence, eventually, but not without being the cause of much grief, transferred to the child, that the cautious and qualified nature of all later relationships must stem?

Before my return to London I had written to the agent who had run the Consort in the old days to see what work was likely to be available. It was possible to approach this agent, since the Consort now worked almost exclusively abroad. The agent offered me a quite gratifying amount of work at first, and in my new mood of confidence I hurried around the country giving recitals, and sometimes playing one-off dates with various ensembles or soloists. But I gradually perceived that the work was not building up. Although it hardly seemed credible that much had changed in only three or four years, I was in fact up against a rapid further development of the fashion for medieval and Renaissance music which, as well as reaching a much wider public, was becoming increasingly dogmatic in matters of technique and style. Records I had made already sounded, even to my ears, 'dated' by comparison with the latest recordings; there was a sweetness and romanticism about them that was no longer admired. It was disconcerting to find my efforts were over-night treated as almost laughable. Of course, I see now this is only to be expected: it is in the normal course of events. I could not hope to swan in and out of the musical scene, finding myself at each entry master of the current situation. I had been spoilt until now, and I found the realization that I would have to adapt, struggle, fight even (I was not afraid of hard work) to build on my former reputation, which my presence did not now assist, immensely galling. For it was not that I myself played any less well, although it might have been reasonable to expect that my personal technique had declined in the years in Heidelberg: it had not. No, it was simply that I had been overtaken by events of an astonishing rapidity. Maybe, if I had been on my own, I would once again have reverted to science, but more probably, come to think of it, I should never have left Heidelberg in the first place. (I was, at this time, still writing up a concluding paper to publish on the rather deadlocked state of my research as I had left it.)

It was unfortunate that just as I had belatedly mastered my stage nerves this much more serious challenge to my viability as a professional musician should arise. After a year of a full diary, engagements had dropped off quite badly. At first it was a treat to be at home with Kiyoko and the child at all sorts of times of day, but after a few weeks when I seemed to have been around for most of the time, Kiyoko raised the subject which I had been trying to push to the back of my mind.

'What are we going to do?' she said. 'I love you being at home, but I suppose it can't go on for ever?' She was by now making a little money herself from Japanese and English translations.

I felt myself losing my temper as a horrible unease and panic swept through me. I jumped up and said to her,

'I don't know what *we* are going to do. *I* am going to try to invent some more work.' And I went out of the room hating myself even as I left, and forced myself to make some phone calls which, in the end, turned up a single date in Manchester (which, however, proved a fruitful connection in that it led to a regular teaching commitment). I could hear, in between calls, Kiyoko putting the little girl to bed, but for the first time I didn't hurry along to see her tucked up into her cot and to listen to Kiyoko singing her to sleep. Much later, then, Kiyoko came to find me. She came straight in and just put herself into my arms, that is, my arms had no option but to put themselves round her as she laid her head on my chest. But nothing would be so easy again.

FOUR

A Musical Adept

I find myself constantly looking and waiting for the 'end' of this story. All sorts of garish and neat devices can be called upon to create an impression of finality. The easiest of all might be the sort of explosion I caused to occur in the laboratory, and which brought an end to the life of my sister. This story could well have stopped there; certainly Fleur's story seemed to – but since then (there is always the tidying-up to do, and before you know where you are you have made a new sort of mess), she has made her existence felt again. We live perhaps in dread and anticipation of the last page. A child to whom you read a bedtime story will anticipate its ending, so much does he want you to read on and on through the night. 'Is that the end?' he will ask anxiously as you turn the page. 'No, not yet!' But when the end does come, he says beseechingly, 'What happened next?' And it is in answer to that, the inappropriate, the wrong, the inartistic question, that I persist in my search for an ending that will not be an end.

It would hardly be an exaggeration to say that Sumi grew up under the piano in the music room. It was there that she thrived. From the earliest days, when she was still only a few months old, whenever she was fretful or restless, the best solution would be to plant her underneath it, in her carry-cot, whereupon if I played she would immediately be calmed. I noticed though that she would not fall asleep – at least, not for a while – but instead lay, her eyes wide open, her little hands waving, with an expression of wonder on her face.

'What do you hear, Sumi?' I would enquire, bending down to look at her under the piano. She did not tell me, but with a vigorous flourish of her hands she asked for more.

By the time she was one year old, and could hold herself upright by clinging on to the piano stool, her demands became more precise. 'Tune, tune!' she would cry, and when I found the one she favoured she laughed with delight. Long before her fingers were strong enough to try to play for themselves, she would insist on sitting on my knee and allowing my hands to carry hers piggy-back up and down the keyboard: together they galloped through preludes and fugues, sonatas and valses. Sometimes the riding hands fell off and had to be retrieved from where they sprawled, helpless with laughter, in a distant octave. By and by I could select a note for her to remember and look out for, and which, at the appointed time, she would strike with all the force she could muster. Soon she learnt to play jokes with her note, and would deliberately mistime it, or misplace it, often with effects that greatly amused her and had to be repeated a hundred times.

But music could also make her sad. It was enough for me to play the first few bars of a certain tune to see her face crumple, her hands fly to her ears; yet sometimes she seemed to want to hear that very tune, for at least as long as she dared to endure such devastating effects.

Before she could talk or knew the names of the notes, Sumi responded to music with music; she would echo the impression it made on her. So if I played for example a thoughtful passage in a minor mode, she would respond with a similar one, which she seemed instinctively and unerringly to seek out by ear, quickly rejecting an inappropriate interval. She could soon imitate and match quite complex rhythmic patterns. It would have been heavy-handed indeed, even as her vocabulary grew, to seek from her a verbal explanation of her response; music played in her and she played with music.

On one of Kiyoko's birthdays, when Sumi was about two and a half years old, we gave what you could call a family recital in her honour. Sumi and I performed our latest 'duet', in which, biting her lips in furious concentration, she firmly and correctly placed at least a dozen notes, and (which impressed me even more) permitted herself no jokes on what was obviously a public occasion. It would have been nice if Kiyoko could have played her fiddle, which at that time she still did with accomplishment, but here I must tell you that there had been an unfortunate development. Sumi, so responsive to music in all its other forms, could not bear the sound of the violin. When Kiyoko played, she would put her hands to her ears and scream. Nothing we could do would assuage her. It was hurtful to Kiyoko who, as I say, still played very well, and made none of the unpleasant sounds that might in the case of some amateur violinist have led one to sympathize with Sumi. I grew to half suspect that it was not in fact just the fiddle that she objected to, but the fact of Kiyoko's playing at all. She would allow her to accompany me without making a fuss, but even then I couldn't help noticing that she reserved her enthusiasm for me, and became rather quiet and unforthcoming to Kiyoko. I tried not to let this situation develop, but Kiyoko not surprisingly was upset by it, and little by little it put her off playing the fiddle.

'I can see there are only to be two musicians allowed in this household,' she remarked acidly, after one such scene, which had ended with my having to take a screaming Sumi away to her room, from which her angry cries still reached us.

'Really, you must try not to mind too much,' I said. 'It's absurd to let a small child's over-sensitivity affect you. You know you play beautifully. We must just ignore her. Come on, let's play the second movement . . .'

But, in practice, it is rather hard to ignore such vigorous and unequivocal comment, and Sumi showed no signs of growing less sensitive or more generous on the subject. Looking back, I am at a loss to know what we, what I, should have done about it. Should I have refused to play with her any more until she accepted that Kiyoko had every right to play as well? It would have been very difficult to make such a crude ruling. And, I fear, the very nature of Sumi's resistance, once evident, was damaging: it was enough that she felt as she did. Perhaps Kiyoko over-reacted? She should have laughed off the prejudice of a mere child? It all happened so gradually that it is impossible to know exactly which of us did too much or too little quite when. But it is clear to me now that slowly Kiyoko withdrew from the music room; the violin case lay unopened for days, weeks, and then months; and it became more and more unusual for her to agree to accompany me. Of course, at the time she seemed perfectly taken up with other things. Her translating was going well, and she had begun to write one or two of her own stories. By the time Sumi was about four years old, anyone calling at the flat and finding us all at home, would have discovered us in what had become our habitual positions: Kiyoko sitting at the Louis Quinze desk, reading or writing; I, practising, or perhaps copying out music, in the music room; and Sumi, depending on what I was up to, either tinkling on the piano or lying underneath it in what she firmly called her playroom, and where her toys and books had accumulated.

Sumi was wise for her years and on the whole behaved with discretion in the music room, where she understood I had serious work to do. She was careful not to be a nuisance to me and rarely played too long or too loudly on, or under, the piano. And I became so used to her presence that if she were not there for any reason, I would look up from my work uneasily, sensing her absence. But one occasion, the first time I was impatient with her, is engraved on my memory. I was deeply immersed in reading the proofs of my long-delayed final paper for the Institut and annoyed already by the amount of sub-editing that had gone on without my permission, when Sumi came running into the room. (The proofs had been dealt with by a young German research assistant, who had first worked for me but since branched out on his own. He had maddened me, but also partly stirred my curiosity, with his suggestions on the proofs, which he had backed up (or so he said) in an accompanying paper which he enclosed, and which I had not yet read.) Sumi had by now already started at the Lycée, and perhaps had just got home; she was wearing her coat.

'Papa, will you take me for a walk?' she asked, coming up and slipping her hand through my arm. I, very distracted, said,

'Not now, Sumi. Run away please. I'm busy.'

But she, unusually for her, was importunate.

'Come on, come on, Papa!' she urged, and she tugged at my elbow.

Irritated out of all proportion, I suddenly spun round, whipping off my spectacles, and snapped at her.

'Go away at once! You can see I'm busy. Leave me alone!'

I was horrified at her reaction. She went quite pale; I had never talked to her in this tone of voice. Her mouth trembled, but she seemed too stunned to cry. She stared at me for a moment as if she couldn't believe her ears, then she shouted,

'I hate you! I hate you!' and turned and ran desperately out of the room.

I threw my paper down in fury and disgust at myself, and wondered what on earth to do. Then I half persuaded myself that she ought to understand by now that she couldn't just interrupt me when she felt like it, and went back to my work. An hour or so later, Kiyoko came in: there seemed to be no peace for me that day.

'What now?' I said.

Kiyoko, who had probably come as a mediator, flinched.

'What can you have said to Sumi?' she asked. 'She is crying her eyes out in her bedroom, and won't speak a word to me.'

'Oh, my God,' I said. 'I simply told her to let me get on with my work. That's all.'

'Yes, well, it is a bit sudden to decide that, isn't it?' said Kiyoko. I was amazed at the coldness in her voice.

'What do you mean?' I demanded.

'You let her spend her whole life in here and then, just because she takes you at your word, you shout at her when you inexplicably don't feel like her any more. No wonder she is hurt!'

'I didn't shout at her!' I now shouted at Kiyoko. 'What's got into you both? I was sitting here, working peacefully – no, not peacefully, I'm struggling with these wretched proofs – when first Sumi expects me to go for a walk with her, and now you blame me for not being able to!'

'You spoil her,' insisted Kiyoko with quite unfamiliar obstinacy, and quite illogically in the present context. We glared at one another. I was the first to come to my senses. I put the proofs away, and got up to go and look for Sumi. Her door was shut, so I tapped on it gently.

'Go away,' said Sumi in a muffled voice.

'Come on out, sweetie,' I said. 'I'm sorry I was cross. But listen, I was very busy. I've got a nasty paper from Germany to read, and it's full of mistakes.'

There was a sort of bumping and scuffling from inside, and eventually Sumi opened the door a crack. I poked my hand round it and made rabbit's ears with my fingers. There was a half-stifled giggle, and the door opened a bit wider.

'But you shouldn't be so cross,' she said reproachfully, when she was once again seated on my knee at the piano. 'I didn't know you could be such a frightening, cross Papa.'

It seems that we at least were friends again.

The news from Dietrich von W. had excited me despite myself. I returned the proofs to him with a brief note of thanks for his conscientious editing, and promised I would try to comment further on the results of his latest work as soon as I had time to examine thoroughly the account of it he had sent me. He had set up a line of experiment under my guidance, but for which I must say I had not held out any great hopes. The results now seemed to have exceeded his most optimistic expectations. I dug out files and papers I thought I had seen the last of, and spent a great deal of energy going, several times, through his figures and analysis. I had not been particularly generous to him as my assistant; our relationship was entirely based on my work – his contribution to which I had formerly treated with scepticism. But when it was, as it now was, clear that he was right, had made the breakthrough he had hoped for – which had far-reaching implications for what I could now only call our line of research, taking it out of the dead end it seemed to have reached – I at once wrote proposing to visit him unofficially to discuss the next steps. He welcomed this. My family did not.

My income from music by now came at least fifty per cent

from visiting teaching posts I held in the music departments of two universities. I arranged for myself to be replaced for the last few weeks of term (von W. and I could not possibly make any headway in less time), made out a large cheque to Kiyoko to cover any unexpected bills, and departed. In the end I stayed away about two months. Von W.'s exposition was brilliant, and his mind was fired with possibilities for the work, possibilities which I had either rejected in the past and which he now rightly reviewed, or had not even imagined.

Towards the end of my stay a letter arrived from Kiyoko, to whom I had spoken several times on the phone but not written at length. Her letter could not have come at a worse moment; I was just wondering if I could arrange (and afford) to stay a third month.

Kiyoko wrote:

'Darling Michael,

It seems silly to write, and I've nothing new to say since we spoke. But you are always in such a hurry on the phone. Do you know when you will be coming back? Several dates have come in, and I am holding them at bay until you decide.

The advance copy of my stories has arrived from Tokyo: it is beautifully printed.

One thing I realize (it is really why I am writing), is that although I miss you, it doesn't really feel any different not having you here – you have been so absent, from me anyway, it seems, for the last year or so. I don't know how this has happened. What do you think?

Sumi of course disagrees, and she adds her note to this letter.'

Sumi had added: 'THE PIANO IS OUT OF TUNE. COME BACK SOON.'

A pattern of recall, as I see more and more, has dominated my life. I cannot honestly say I have chosen to do one thing or the other; rather I have been impelled, in a cycle of by now, you may feel, predictable events, to drop what I am doing and take up its replacement. I am, as it were, pinioned to a medieval wheel of fortune which spins me ineluctably in and out of the worlds of science and music. The people I have loved (they are very few) also move in and out of my sphere of consciousness: it seems there is nothing I can do about it. If I had become 'absent' from Kiyoko, she too had become absent from me. For what she said in her letter was true, although I could not find an answer for her that would have served any purpose.

But nevertheless, at the sight of Sumi's imperious capitals I resolved to go home. Von W. would have to get on without me. Perhaps, even, he would be relieved by my departure; after all, he was in charge from now on. He saw me off at the station with his usual mixture of formality and courtesy.

'My regards, Herr Doktor, to your wife,' he said, with that little old-fashioned bow, restricted these days just to the head, that ducks sharply as if a hand has grasped the back of the coat-collar.

'Keep me in touch,' I said. 'Goodbye.'

On the journey home from Heidelberg I re-read Kiyoko's letter and tried to make some practical suggestions to myself as to what I could do to improve matters between us. Sumi loomed large, but imprecisely, in my thoughts; I knew that in some way I did not care to examine her role in Kiyoko's and my detachment from one another. Was it not, if anything, Kiyoko's fault if she chose to leave us so much together? She had abandoned the music room and devoted herself to her writing. I reassured myself with the thought that Sumi would anyway soon be going to school full time, which would help to make her more independent.

And to some extent this proved to be so. Once she was a schoolgirl, Sumi naturally ceased to live in the music room; I was often away from home (one of the university jobs was in the north of England), and our meetings were restricted to afternoon music lessons when I was there, and occasional evenings together at the piano. I continued to teach her for several years, although 'teaching' becomes a qualified term when the pupil is so exceptionally self-taught; it is rather a matter of judiciously guiding and prompting an intelligence or talent as it forges its own way. Perhaps from time to time it leaps, like a goat, on to a rock that is perched above a precipice rather than leading on up its intended path. Your job as teacher is then as it were to wave from the path (hold out the safety net); quick as a flash, it turns in its flight and re-lands neatly. Then, before you can congratulate yourself, or even give a sigh of relief, it has bounded off and away. I felt as if I were always puffing uphill in pursuit of Sumi. She would arrive in my room like a whirlwind, dropping her school books and her coat before I had time to take off my spectacles.

She usually began by playing her latest piece, learnt perhaps since her last lesson, while I had been away. Her repertoire was growing rapidly; at eight she could play from memory about a dozen pieces, which she selected (after I had played them to her) from the pile of music that had belonged to Fleur, and to which I had added over the years. The music had come in a large chest with the piano from the family house. Sumi would rummage through it, looking for something that appealed to her. Soon we needed to order new music, and one of the greatest excitements in her life would be the arrival of a package from a music publisher. When we had decided on a piece to learn, I would write her name in the top right-hand corner; sometimes this would be under Fleur's proprietary flourish. It was not surprising then that Sumi became curious about her predecessor at the piano.

'Was she good? as good as I am?'

'You mean at playing the piano?'

'Of course!'

'She was very talented. But no, I think not as good as you will be. Anyway, she hadn't got so far before she died.'

'How did she die?'

Only this subject could divert Sumi from her music lesson.

'In an accident. Don't let's talk about it.'

But one day this line of questioning took another turn. Sumi, about eleven years old by now, sat down at the piano as usual, but didn't open her music. Instead she looked gravely and consideringly at me, in an unnatural silence, until I raised my eyebrows at her enquiringly.

Sumi frowned, turned away for a moment, then looked back at me.

'Did you love your sister?' she asked determinedly.

'Of course,' I replied. I reached to open the piece (it was by Debussy) that she had elected to learn.

'No,' she said, suddenly and fiercely. I sat back, trying not to think what could be coming. I felt curiously inert and unresistant, but I forced myself to try to divert her again.

'Sumi, please, you know that isn't my favourite subject. I don't want to talk about it,' I said with an effort. I might as well have been trying to silence Fleur herself.

'She loved you, and you loved her, properly. Like grown-ups?' said Sumi, but it was a statement, not a question.

I looked at her in silence for a while. I wondered dimly how she could possibly know (Kiyoko would never have told her) – and then, pulling myself together, what she knew? What did she mean by 'properly'? Was she just acting out of some sort of possessive instinct?

'That was a long time ago,' I said at last.

'Papa, don't pretend. I know,' said Sumi. And she handed me the exercise book in which my sister Fleur had written her 'Memoirs' that summer before she died. You have read them already; I have placed them earlier in this story, at the point when it seemed most interesting (amusing even) to hear from her. But in fact it was only now that they surfaced. You may have wondered where they had been; where they had come from. It seems then that Fleur had left the book quite carelessly amongst her music (perhaps intending to hide it later), and Sumi, on one of her rummages, which grew more thorough as the search for new music grew more critical, had unearthed it from the piece by Debussy which now stood on the piano.

'What is it?' I asked Sumi at first, glancing at the exercise book. 'Don't say you have turned into an author too?'

But she shook her head impatiently, and so I began to read more carefully. I saw soon enough what it was.

'No lesson today, then,' I said. 'You want me to read this?'

Sumi got up reluctantly, but before she went away she suddenly snatched up my free hand and held it against her cheek; then she had gone, and I was left to read Fleur's account of herself. I hardly noticed that day what she wrote, that is, I took no interest in her version, so meaningless, so wasteful now it was all too late. All my attention was bent on trying to see what it could possibly have meant to Sumi: how had she understood it? Then I wondered whether I should tell Kiyoko what had happened, and ask her to try to explain, but I decided I could not face that, at least not yet. Better to try to have a brief talk with Sumi myself, and put things into perspective. I realized I'd have to tell her a little about the accident to help her make sense of the story.

The next day, when she got back from school, I suggested

to her that we go for a walk. She knew at once what this meant, and joined me at the door.

'Where are you off to?' called Kiyoko from her desk.

'We're going for a walk,' I called back, feeling, with a sinking heart, like a conspirator.

How tall Sumi had grown! As we walked through the park I noticed her head was already nearly on a level with my shoulder.

'You're going to be taller than Kiyoko,' I said to her. Her hair was cut these days into a typical Japanese style, with a square fringe and shoulder-length bob, and she looked, the older she became, and as her cheeks grew paler, more Japanese and less English, less like Fleur.

But now she told me that she was like Fleur, that she loved me as much as Fleur had done, only much more, and much better.

'I love you properly, Papa!' she said, with a pathetic anxiety in her voice, as if she knew I would not believe her. 'I wouldn't want to hurt you like she did. She blamed you, but I can see it was all her fault!'

Where could I begin, or rather, where could I make an end, as swift and painless an end as possible, to this?

We sat down on a bench and I told her as calmly and factually as I could about Fleur's and my childhood, about my experiments in the laboratory, and the fatal explosion. The Will, I explained, and the Marriage (even the grown-up bits) had been part of one of Fleur's complicated games, did she understand? But all the time I had the feeling that my words were quite meaningless to Sumi, that she was waiting for me to finish only out of politeness.

'But we love one another now,' was all she said at the end, as if my account of the past was of no relevance any more.

'Of course we do, I am your father,' I said illogically.

And then Sumi put her face up to mine and kissed me.

Has anyone described the kiss of a child? I have searched my memory for an account that I could resort to, that might be of some use to me, that I could at least amend, or contradict, or perhaps, if it seemed just, comfortably affirm. I will search in my head, anyway, for everything that it is not: it is not a light-hearted, careless, and uncommitted courtesy, a formula of the adult world that a child feels bound to imitate while despising it a little in his or her heart, a mere brush with distracted humanity; it is not a passionless and unphysical thing.

Sumi had always been a demonstrative child; she sprang at us and hugged us, and when she was younger and we kissed her goodnight in bed she would put her arms round our necks and try to drag us down until, off balance, we toppled over on to her and she held us, prisoner, in her arms. This she did to Kiyoko as much as to me, though Kiyoko would protest and rise, rather ruffled, from the fray. I tended to succumb more easily.

Now, when she kissed me, it was as if she placed, with the pressure of her child's salty mouth, her whole life on my lips. But I will not go on. It is impossible to speak of without doing offence to it. Yet she gazed at me as if she expected me to speak.

'Sumi, darling,' I said, in a mixture of confusion at her vehemence, terror at my own feelings which I could not possibly pause to consider, and a frantic desire to be gentle with her.

'Sumi, that is not for me. Listen, you are in a muddle. You mustn't love me too much, not that much. I'm here to look after you, you'll learn to do without me as you get older.'

Perhaps that sounds like an absurdly inflated response (and perhaps I may not have said it like that, not all at once), but then you did not receive her kiss. And even then that was not gentle enough, did not take her seriously enough, for Sumi, in a despair as passionate as her declaration, now leapt to her feet.

'You think I'm a child,' she cried. 'But I shall love you for ever! Far better than Fleur, or even than Kiyoko can do!'

Imagine these words on the lips of an adult, a jealous mistress, or a rejected lover! Ridiculous indeed. And for a moment I almost wanted to laugh at her. Sometimes I wish I had; she would have been bitterly hurt, but might it not have been just the rebuff she needed? But instead (was it out of a vanity just as ridiculous?) I am afraid I took her at her word.

'It must be different,' I think I said. 'We must make sure it is different, Sumi.' But I knew she had no hope of understanding me yet. 'Perhaps I make it difficult for you. I teach you; we see too much of one another.' But this was misguided. Sumi looked at me wildly.

'You won't send me away? I'll die if I have to go away, or if you stop teaching me!' she said.

'Darling, you won't die,' I said firmly. 'And one day quite soon, anyway, you will have to have a new and much better teacher than I am if your playing is to progress. You know that, we've discussed it already.' I was grateful for this practical diversion.

'Not yet,' said Sumi and (we were by now walking along the path, and I was trying to turn homewards) she stopped again and confronted me. I looked down at her: love, and what she thought of as desire, her ambitiousness as a musician, the beginnings of the anxiety of someone who is suddenly leaving their childhood behind them, all struggled confusedly in her face, which I now stroked gently. But all I could see my way to doing was to extract from her a promise to be 'good and sensible'. I left her at the front door, and went off on some invented errand of my own.

And so began that sad withdrawal of a parent from the physical life of its child. Usually, of course, it starts on the signals of modesty and embarrassment from the child, as it becomes aware of itself, and rightly desires to be private, signals which are properly respected by the more casual, immodest adult. But in Sumi's case, it was I that now chose, against her wishes, to make fewer inroads into her personal life. It was easy to do, since she was of an age when I would anyway have stopped, for instance, walking freely in and out of the bathroom when she was there; I no longer perched on her bed with unquestioning ease. I soon brought up the matter of the new piano teacher, which was of genuine necessity, and Sumi, wisely allowing her ambitions in that field to dictate to her, and perhaps out of a dull awareness that she was anyway to be outmanoeuvred, responded to the plan with docility, if not quite the enthusiasm I would formerly have expected.

If Kiyoko observed this and drew any conclusion, she gave no signs of doing so, and indeed, if I write now only about Sumi, it is partly because Kiyoko had ceased to comment. Or could I, simply, no longer hear her comments? One acts, one writes, one falls in love, when what is attractive and uppermost in life suddenly corresponds with what is most deeply rooted in one's nature. In between the almost fortuitous object and the obsessional, layers of shallow thoughts and feelings ply vaguely to and fro, sometimes useful, sometimes irrelevant, always powerless against the strength of obsessional attention. If I was now bound to recall Fleur in every step that Sumi took, that at least could be explained in these terms. But from where had Sumi derived her feelings? Not, surely, from the reading of the 'Memoirs', which had merely precipitated her declaration; not from any past of her own. Sometimes I wondered guiltily if it was all my fault, whether somehow the facts of my own history had irresistibly attracted my helpless daughter;

whether my own obsession, like a sort of odour, persisted about me, which Sumi, in some indefinable way, was now bound to sense and respond to. When I thought like this, I became so terrified that I thought the best thing I could do would be to remove myself at once from her life. But in a more rational frame of mind it occurred to me that my extreme reaction was absurd and unnecessary. It was possible to argue after all that her attraction was quite 'natural', even if social mores made it impossible. We have, by dint of social taboos, made monsters of ourselves. A young child, not yet permeated with our traditions, our scruples, may act instinctively in expressing what seems to him or her to be an entirely natural affection.

But then, unable to feel any differently so far as I myself was concerned, I developed a theory of responsibility. It was a matter of power once again: a father (or a teacher) may not use his natural power over his daughter to such an end. She could too easily be perverted against her wish to his will. But if she, the daughter, seemed to ask and invite, what then? This certainly undermined the argument, but no, for such a form of susceptibility was almost to be expected: it sprang from the inevitable, innocent, and not to be exploited desire to please. No adult could consent to such an unequal relationship! And so I fought back at myself, almost as if I had allowed myself to admit the existence of this situation. For if I had, where could it lead?

And only then, belatedly, did it occur to me that it led me, must lead me, to Kiyoko.

FIVE

Broken Consort

Kiyoko

Sometimes I wonder if I have ever forgiven Michael for those days in Paris when he refused to talk to me. A great deal has happened since then: why! we re-met, fell in love at last or again, married, and had a child. But perhaps for as long as the last ten of the fifteen years we have lived together, we have merely re-enacted those early visits to my rooms. Could there be, at the heart of this failure, an old rankling?

First impressions are rarely altogether false, though they may be inadequate: sooner or later, you will recognize what you glimpsed and believed then, good and bad. But what would be my first impression of Michael? It is, they are, entirely mixed. Very first of all, it is not his eyes sliding sideways from mine as he kneels on my tea mat that I recall, but rather his sweet sudden smile as I was turning the page at the second desk of violins. The smile came first; only later his eyes slipped evasively sideways. The smile returned for a while in Heidelberg. It has been gone from me for a long time now. Only Sumi can recapture it.

Sweetness is not a characteristic men pride themselves on, but in Michael (though he is never conscious of it) it is a foremost quality. I can imagine, as I insist on the word, how he would object. 'Men are not "sweet",' he would say mockingly. (Japanese and English men 'do not cry' either.) I have even spent some time, as if to pre-empt his criticism, looking the word up so at least I will not be guilty of that sort of misattribution. In fact the dictionary flies to my rescue: to be 'sweet' is to be pleasing to the senses especially of taste and smell; it is (of water) to be fresh, not salt; and in Old Chemistry, to be free from corrosive salt, sulphur and acid. It is, too, to be pleasing to the ear: musical, melodious, harmonious; it is to be dearly loved, precious, dear . . .

When I wonder if I have not forgiven him for those early difficult days, I do not refer to my uppermost feelings, with which I swept away all obstacles to our eventually loving one another. But is it possible to allay an anguish that has lodged, deep down, despite yourself, despite everything you mean and want now? Once we were at odds; we were alien. However closely you approach and mitigate since, does the memory of separateness ever quite go? and while there is memory must there not be again and again the unresolved pain? I know of no cure for this.

When my brother finished his course in Paris and returned to Tokyo leaving me on my own in the rooms we had shared until then (he helped me convince our parents that I would be all right on my own in Paris), I lived at first a very solitary life. The friends I had made through my brother, mostly art students like himself, had either left Paris at the same time as he or, in the case of Japanese students, a certain diffidence and formality made them shy of seeing me once I was on my own. I spoke absurdly little French by then, having relied too much on my brother's greater expertise. At the Conservatoire it was easy to come and go to lessons and rehearsals with little personal contact. So when Michael smiled at me, I was pleased out of all proportion. I had noticed him already, a quite tall, fair English boy, with thick hair that sprang energetically upwards from his brow, unexpectedly contrasting dark eyebrows, and green eyes; and who affected to smoke a pipe. He looked like a mixture of a philosopher and a clown. Only he did not tumble and laugh; he was very still. And, I had noticed, solitary too, although he was attractive enough not to need to be. He was careful, once we had met, in a way other young men were not. He would appear at my side and take my case from me without a word, escort me home, buy me coffee in rehearsal breaks – silently he began to look after me, even to assume my presence, or his presence by my side. I felt I was no longer alone. But curiously our friendship went no further. I would make tea for him and try to open up the conversation, but then it was that his eyes would grow distant and slide half-mockingly from mine, as he pretended he could not understand what I was trying to say. Courteously enough, he would take his leave. But sometimes I knelt on a long while after he had gone and cried into the tea; and eventually, when I felt I had cried too much, I told myself I had misinterpreted his concern and I no longer asked him home.

Then I learnt he was going out with a French girl who was said to be very clever, an 'intellectual'; and soon afterwards I met the man with whom I was to live, and to whom I was married for a while.

Just before I went to Germany I had considered returning to Japan. My parents, growing old, were trying to persuade me to go home; even my brother, by now a successful painter, tried to convince me I was needed there. But although things had not gone very well for me, I was too used to my independent European way of life to be able to imagine fitting in in the East again.

A few years before we re-met (at about the same time, Michael told me later, that he was enquiring after me at the

Embassy in Paris), I saw in a shop window some records made by an English Consort, with Michael's name on the sleeve. I went in at once, and bought several, including his solo recording of the Bach gamba sonatas, which was already quite worn out by the time I moved to Mannheim. I knew of Michael only as a musician, and was startled, disconcerted even, to find he was also, or as it seemed then, instead, a physicist.

'But how can that be? I have always thought of you as a musician! Why, I even have several of your records,' I told him at the Heidelberg reception.

'Well, not any more. Not professionally, anyway,' he replied. 'I have always, at least since I was about sixteen, had the two lines.' And he asked me about my own playing.

'I have kept it up, but only as an amateur,' I admitted.

'I too,' he said. 'Perhaps we can play trios one evening? Would you like to meet our pianist?' He steered me across the room to talk to a friend of his. I recognized his habit of withdrawing from the thick of the conversation, as now he stood back and seemed to be concentrating on mending the stem of his pipe rather than watching or listening to us. But when I eventually glanced, perhaps rather appealingly, at him, he at once stepped forward to the rescue and took my elbow; within a quarter of an hour we had left the reception and were going out to supper together.

'No trios this evening!' he said firmly. How talkative he proved after all!

Eight years had gone by, and we had had, it seems, no choice but to waste them apart from one another. If we had known that we could waste years that we were to spend together, what would we have found to say that evening?

It was only when my brother went back to Japan that he partly retrieved, partly found his own convincing style. To observe his progress in Paris was like watching a speeded-up film of European art history. I still have on my wall, above my French desk, a vague and shimmery watercolour of the Parc Monceau, *style impressioniste*, that he gave me when I first came to Paris. I was only just in time. A month later the park was laid out in cubist slabs and blocks; soon afterwards it was the scene of a surrealist defloration; and by the end of the year it had reformed yet again as a structuralist zone in which a tree was not even a memory. I found myself revisiting it secretly to reassure myself that it remained impervious to my brother's palette. But who am I to mock? The repertoire at the Conservatoire was immutably fixed, and besides I was not a composer. It was only when I began to write children's stories in a language that is not my own that the problems of influences became clear to me. To be faithful to one's own culture, and to respond at the same time to the exigencies of a foreign language requires a very delicate sense of balance. The rather garish and even violent action that would be acceptable in a Japanese tale, for instance, has to take on the guise of a more surrealist fantasy to remain convincing in an English story. But both Japanese and English seem to have a down-to-earth quality in common, which contrasts with the more melodramatic vein. Action strikes unreasonably; the characters regard it and deal with it practically. But by now I may only be justifying my own particular mixture. Michael used to object to the strange events in my stories: 'But why?' he demanded. 'It's so improbable!' 'It's really too much!' And I know sometimes he is right; I go too far. Until you have tried to do without such violent effects you have not begun to face the real problems of thinking and writing. I came to find the expression on Sumi's face quite a useful gauge. If she looked a little uneasy and doubtful, I was probably right to be worried; if she looked confident and approving, I could be reassured.

Michael

How often the thing we most want or need to know, or the person to whom we most need to turn (or who most needs us), is so near that we only have to open one eye or put out a hand to see or touch them – but that is exactly what we seem least able to do. From the moment that I knew I should turn to Kiyoko, and failed to do so, I count myself guilty. Until now, however much I was to blame, I could at least ascribe my behaviour to confusion or ignorance (as a boy), or to a sort of desperately well-intentioned passivity since. I took, as I have described, measures to remove myself gently and by degrees from Sumi's personal life. We never referred to our talk, and she did not appear to seek me out. I resolved that I would not allow opportunities to arise when she could be tempted to re-introduce the subject. So gradually I deceived myself into thinking I could change, or for ever deflect, the latent situation.

I write, I realize, as if nothing else happened in our lives, as if we saw no other people, as if world events withdrew when they heard us coming, and the planets froze in their tracks. Countries went to war; millions of refugees were hounded around the world; other millions starved with annual precision. At some point about this time, my father astonished us all by giving the greater part of the money he had inherited from my grandparents towards the formation of a new political party in Britain. It was not in fact very much money: a sum that had seemed enormous to Fleur and me when we scrutinized grandfather's Will, but only respectable to my parents when they saw the need to reduce grandmother's living expenses, had further dwindled in thirty years of inflation and over-conservative investment. Nevertheless, it was a gesture which distressed my mother, largely I think on my behalf, since she had never forgiven me for leaving my well-paid German post and now saw me even further condemned to the life of a penurious musician.

But my father was acting only in the best tradition of his forebears. At the beginning of the century my great-grandfather had given a far more significant sum to Keir Hardie. It should not be seen as ironic – though I suppose many will see it so – that my father now supported a move remote from socialism as Hardie had conceived of it, but rather as the same altruistic instinct at work, encouraging the desire and need for change that would suit the times. My great-grandfather had as a young man in Germany been one of the first to promote worker-management in the family factory he owned on the edges of the Black Forest. But as a liberal at the time of Bismarck, he had found life in Germany unendurable; he had left the country and expressed his disaffection further in personal terms by marrying a French girl (the music student, you will recall) around the time that France was forced to cede Alsace and East Lorraine to Germany. From then on he found no practical outlet for his political views; he lived in Switzerland and then England, where he published books on the public ownership of land; and finally, despairing of the future of socialism in Europe, he had emigrated to New Zealand.

Grandfather had, it seems, taken no active interest in politics, but immured in his laboratory in the Home Counties he had held increasingly conservative views, and certainly he brought up his son (my father) as a conservative Englishman, who appeared to know very little of his European past, which perhaps he had learnt to be wary of since he had had to fight as a boy in defence of his suspect name. So it was, as I say, surprising to us when he suddenly decided, unapologetically, to make this explicit political gesture.

'You will receive a little money on my death, but don't bank on it. It will be worth even less by then,' he said rather curtly to me.

'Certainly I don't "bank" on it,' I replied equally drily. 'It would be nice to know that there is enough to provide for Mama, that's all?'

'Of course,' snapped my father.

I tried to involve him in political discussion: what were his ideals and hopes for the prospective party, whose aims I must admit seemed tenuous to me, but he refused to be drawn. He seemed, simply, to feel that things could not go on as they were, and a middle party seeking a realignment on a classless basis must by definition be an improvement on the moribund status quo (only it needed money from somewhere). It was an unsophisticated case, and would doubtless have been the despair of our Continental ancestor.

In Heidelberg, von W.'s development of my research had also contributed to the march of history; an even more lethal and refined potentiality would soon make its way into the hands of certain wealthy governments. Von W. was now working, belatedly some would say, on a method of reversing his development: he found it difficult to raise money for this stage of his research. Despite his success, he had remained surprisingly deferential; he kept me well informed, and consulted me regularly. I visited him at intervals, but resisted several offers from the Institut to return on a more permanent basis.

The penultimate decade of the twentieth century was upon us, and you would think there would be more to write about than a little girl, however talented, whose name was Sumi.

But Sumi was of course no longer such a little girl. For four years she had continued her lessons with a Russian pianist, who as I had predicted, had transformed her playing. I flattered myself that I had given her a good grounding in technique, and in repertoire, yet her new teacher took her right back to the beginning, and altered several things to do with the angle of her wrist, the approach of her fingers, and so on. She now practised for about four or five hours a day, before breakfast and going to the Lycée, and again on her return in the late afternoon. Her style, her touch, was a distinctive mixture of vigour and confidence tempered by a delicacy and refinement which she had acquired from her teacher, whose own playing was of exceptional delicacy for a man's. And she still brought to her playing the sense of humour she had shown from her earliest days at the keyboard.

All three of us were so busy that I was willingly lulled into thinking Sumi had grown resigned, indeed had been diverted, had grown out of her misguided feelings for me. I thought (if I thought about it at all any more) that the bad moment had passed, and that I should never have to worry Kiyoko. A house with two busy artists in it is bad enough; one with three is even more complicated. More and more often, for instance, I found myself driven out of the music room; a gamba can be carried into a next-door bedroom, a piano can hardly be moved so easily. Kiyoko's typewriter dominated the kitchen; it was to be seen on the table more regularly than meals. She went abroad on several visits, to France and to Japan, and on those occasions I made sure we invited someone to live in and keep house for us. Sumi too went away several summers running to a music summer-school where she made her début, playing first a Haydn and then a Mozart concerto with student orchestras. Altogether we were so busy we hardly had a moment to stop to think about either the outside world, or, on the contrary, our inner selves.

Kiyoko, I said earlier, had 'ceased to comment'. And if I stop and force myself to think about it, I realize that my last positive sight of her was as she leant against the doorpost talking about the 'irresistible' Allegro so many years ago. Then she was herself entire. Certainly I have described her since then – sitting at the newly-presented Louis Quinze desk, for instance, or giving birth to Sumi – but those impressions, however vivid, are strangely modified in my mind: it is as though there had been a re-arrangement of elements; the addition of a certain agent had acted like a catalyst upon us. If we ignore the Louis Quinze desk (an inanimate object may surely not play such an important part in a human story), then it is easy to deduce that we are left with Sumi. At about this time, seeing how independent Kiyoko's life had become, I made a transparent attempt to draw her back into our musical orbit. I proposed that, for fun, we should form a family 'broken consort'. Kiyoko would have had to promise to practise seriously again, and we could have borrowed a harpsichord I knew of. But this was a futile gesture. Kiyoko no longer wished to resume playing the fiddle, and Sumi didn't particularly want to play the harpsichord. They both looked at me, half-amused, and shrugged their shoulders.

And Kiyoko's own work? At first she had tested stories on Sumi. In the early years I too might be treated to an experimental night-time story last thing in bed, and I was sometimes helpful over matters such as improbable endings, or incorrect English. But what had formerly been fiery and entertaining discussions had degenerated into rather pedantic intrusions on my part, and Kiyoko, as she grew more experienced, and her English improved until it was really as good as a native English speaker's (though with occasional bizarre and charming lapses), consulted me less and less.

We had thought at first of having a second child. Yet for no particular or good reason this became imperceptibly postponed, until suddenly it seemed 'too late'; we were both too busy to start again. It would have been too disruptive.

I don't know that it is possible to detect, let alone to describe, the slow elapse of a marriage. It is more a matter of occasional, abrupt perceptions of ground that is already irretrievably eroded. For a time you have been walking carelessly on a dune that is threaded together with tough marram grass; then your foot plunges (wrenching your ankle) into a gaping hole from which the sand is pouring away. A child might rush to and fro packing the hole with new damp sand from the beach, slapping it firm with his spade, and prepared to stand on guard by it till nightfall; the more wary adult catches his breath and sidesteps to firmer ground.

We were not, though, apparently negligent of one another. Despite the presence of the typewriter on the kitchen table, meals did appear (I was I must admit rather playing with words when I suggested earlier that they were comparatively irregular); Kiyoko was a meticulous and graceful housewife. The flat was quite sparsely furnished and, despite its European contents, always managed to have what I imagined was an oriental atmosphere: it was arranged on cool and delicate lines. I, as I was at home as much or as little as she, took my turn with the shopping and cooking. It was not then a matter of selfish disregard for domestic routine. Deep down, somewhere you cannot penetrate, our, or perhaps only my, concentration had slipped.

I am saying, am I not, that I no longer loved Kiyoko.

But if I admitted that (for no! I have not), what then could be said for 'love'? Had I only felt for her a passionate gratitude? She had come into my life when I cared for nothing and given herself to me without question. I had allowed myself to take her. It was clear, years later, that I had conspicuously failed to 'make love'.

Kiyoko

What can I do to avert the course our lives are taking? We work, all three of us, harder and harder; we move in and out of one another's presence like haunted creatures – haunted by the memory of our former existence together. Each day Michael's deliberate formality with Sumi brings her to the verge of tears; he pretends not to notice, perhaps genuinely doesn't. And if I speak to him, I am shocked by the coldness in my voice and fall silent as quickly as I can, sometimes before I even finish what I meant to say. The air is sharp with the frost of half-finished sentences, unexplained and unresolved dilemmas.

I have been wondering recently whether I should not, after all these years, return to Japan. My last visit there was very successful; my publisher tried hard to persuade me to stay. And then, too, there is the temptation of working with Y-, the painter whom I met through my brother, on the series of stories we have been commissioned to do together. I felt, working with him, such a sense of relief, as if the struggle to express myself in a foreign context has somehow been unnecessary. While I have been wrestling with self-imposed artificial and alien problems, Y- has understood exactly what I meant to say and how I should say it; his brush expresses it before I have hardly begun to write (but he says he did not know what his brush could express before I began to write). And since that visit, Michael and our life in London have seemed effortful and ungiving in quite a new and serious way.

I do not know how one can go back to drudgery after such glimpses. But what would Sumi make of Japan? It could not be a less propitious moment to move her. She is far advanced with the Baccalauréat syllabus, and she works well with her piano teacher. I made tentative enquiries about teachers in Tokyo, but I know I am deceiving myself. It would not be right for her to move. Her whole training has been in the European mould, and the Japanese emphasis on comparatively superficial pianistic brilliance would not suit her at all, might positively harm her now. And then, of course, she would refuse to be separated from Michael.

But what of Sumi and Michael? The past will not leave us alone to make our lives as we long to. For us there is no easy solution, no mere 'forgiveness', no finishing and starting again. I speak largely of Michael's past, for in our context it has proved the least innocent, the least able to be changed. We mislead ourselves when we think, momentarily, our understanding can transform what has happened. At first perhaps Michael feared that by confusing me with Fleur he would lose me – at the time I must have seemed his best chance – and somehow in Heidelberg he was strong enough to fight for our survival together. It was not difficult for me to understand him then. Had I not loved my brother above everyone? If anything I envied Fleur her courage – but I did not dwell on that, and indeed it would have been perverse to do so, since things had gone so very wrong for them. But later I realized that my understanding had been for nothing; it had not helped Michael in the long run. Sumi stepped over me into his life and resumed the story at the point Fleur had discontinued it. And ridiculously I began to envy her, to fight a losing battle with her – a little child, my daughter!

I suppose I knew I had lost, not when Sumi was small and they were so openly happy and enchanted with one another, but when they began to conceal their love. From the day that Michael called to me from the front door saying they were 'going for a walk' in that absurdly offhand way, as if he were embarking on a clandestine engagement with a mistress, I knew I could no longer deflect them. But I think something must have happened between them around then, for Michael began to be much more careful not to spend so much time with Sumi. He became more remote, and has cultivated, as I said, a formality with her that hurts her terribly. She cannot understand it, and in her confusion she often turns resentfully on me when he has, as it were, held her at arm's length. But she probably does not realize how little I have come to mean to him; it is not I that lie, ever-watchful, in between.

And if I did, I would know that I cannot keep them apart indefinitely. Should I, for this reason too, go away, or am I bound above all on this account to stay and watch?

Michael

In the late summer of 1980 Kiyoko announced that another trip was in the offing; she was expected to go to Tokyo at rather short notice to work on a new series of children's books with her enthusiastic and faithful publisher and an artist collaborator. She mentioned, tentatively, that it might even become a good idea for her to live in Japan for a while: had either of us considered this as a possibility? Sumi and I were aghast. Although Sumi was quite curious to visit what was after all one of her countries of origin, she could not entertain the thought of leaving her studies at this point, and particularly her teacher. I think I was glad to see how much she admired him, how dependent on him she had become. As for myself, I could not imagine what I could do in Japan: how would I earn a living? Kiyoko said vaguely I could probably teach somewhere, but she agreed, equably enough, that it was too much to expect us both to uproot ourselves. She left, seen off by her British publisher at the airport.

No one was free to housekeep for us this time, so Sumi and I agreed we would have to manage on our own. I would cook, if she was willing to do the shopping. We seemed to cope quite well between us, though we missed the clatter of the typewriter in the kitchen. Kiyoko had been away for about a week when it dawned on me that Sumi was behaving oddly. At first I pretended not to notice when in the evenings she began, for instance, to make a special effort to look particularly pretty. She would change, quite unnecessarily, before our informal enough suppers, and one evening I found her, in an absurdly would-be sophisticated pose, smoking at the kitchen table. I opened the window and pointedly emptied the ashtray. Sumi blushed with mortification, but did not say a word.

'I thought that was Kiyoko's kimono,' I said, feeling I had gone too far, which was stupid of me. Sumi grew more confident.

'Isn't it lovely?' she said. 'Kiyoko never wears it. I don't think she'd mind my trying it on.' And she stood up and spun round slowly, so I could admire it, and her. The kimono was exquisite, and I could not help but see that my daughter had grown beautiful. She was taller than Kiyoko, as I had predicted she would be; she had slanted eyes the colour of a tiger's-eye stone, and fine black eyebrows in a face that had recently grown thinner, perhaps from tiredness; she worked too hard.

'What have you bought for supper?' I asked irritably, to distract myself. All evening she seemed particularly solicitous; she waited on me, and cleared away with unusual grace. The quieter and more adept she grew, the more restless and uneasy I became, until I visibly jumped when she brought me a cup of coffee at my desk in the music room. She then offered to play to me, and as I watched her and listened I became more and more aware that we were on our own, as I had resolved we never should be. Last of all, after hunting for a while in the music chest, she produced Debussy's 'La Fille aux cheveux de lin'. When she began to play it, I stood up, half meaning to stop her, but she (while the right hand played the tentative and dreamy opening bars) raised her left forefinger at me. I sank back into my chair and buried my face in my hands. I hoped I would never look up again, but when at last, it seemed much later, I raised my head, Sumi had undressed and stood in front of me. I can't say I was surprised to see her there. I took her by the hand and went with her, or she with me, we went together, without waiting any longer, to her room.

A few nights later Kiyoko returned unannounced and found us. Had we forgotten her existence? What can we have wanted to happen? Kiyoko stood briefly in the doorway of Sumi's room, and then went into the kitchen where she waited for me to get up and join her. We agreed at once that she should re-depart for Japan, with Sumi, as soon as possible.

In the autumn I went back to Heidelberg, to cause trouble for von W. for another term.

In 1965 it had seemed to me that against all the odds I had witnessed a resurrection from the dead. In 1980 there was no hope of resurrecting that much more desirable thing, the living. My wife and daughter now lived six thousand miles away from me; I heard nothing from them. It was clear to me I could never expect to see them again. I accepted the post, repeatedly pressed on me at Heidelberg; my instruments I left in London: I had no more use for them. The Louis Quinze desk met its belated end on a bonfire on a building site; I burnt it, delicate leg by leg, little drawer by drawer. No one came to put a stop to this deranged and destructive gesture. I left it smouldering, the black lacquer peeling as it melted. Half-stifled by the fumes from the much-treated wood, I stumbled away. It was harder from then on to tell what was the worst thing I had ever done.

SIX

Notes from Sumi

Paris 17ᵉ
11 March 1982

It is my seventeenth birthday. I have not seen Papa for almost eighteen months, and I'm not even sure if he knows we are living here now. Mama and I spent the first few months in Tokyo, where we stayed with her family (mine too, I suppose), but when I was better she decided it would be much easier for me to continue my French schooling, and so we moved to Paris. I go to the Lycée nearby. I had missed a term, but my French marks from London were good enough to let me go on into the Ière classe and finish the Baccalauréat this year.

I was ill in Tokyo. At school my case is explained as a 'crise de nerfs', almost to be expected in a growing-up musician, and justified even more by the fact that my parents have separated. I hardly played the piano in Japan, but since we came to Paris I have started again. My London teacher made sure I was taken on by a good teacher at the Conservatoire, where I have been enrolled while still at school.

People ask me about Japan, but I can't tell them much. I looked at very little while we were there. My relations were puzzled by me, and Kiyoko had a dreadful time avoiding explanations. She has been very kind to me. It is curious but over the last year I have almost stopped thinking of her as my mother. She has become more of a friend and ally, although we say quite little to one another. The only time we talked directly about what happened and Mama asked me specific questions, rather like a doctor, was before we left England. (Papa had already left the flat; I don't know where he'd gone.) I understand now that she was very worried. You see, it is difficult for me to say, but she had no idea what the consequences for me might be. But I realized that Papa had of course been very careful of me. He always had been; how could he not be now? I was dreadfully afraid for him, not for me. Kiyoko's questions upset me more than anything. I hated her for asking them. 'You've no right to speak, Mama,' I shouted at her that day. 'You never have spoken. You were not even there!' I didn't mean this literally; I don't know what I meant, but Kiyoko looked as if I had hit her.

But since then I see she thought she needed to ask me. I have started to watch her, and perhaps to see her properly for the first time. I know Papa always thought she was very beautiful, and now I see he was right (I didn't like to think of this before): she is very slim – her bones are as fine as a bird's, and her movements are light and graceful. I am taller and rather heavier. And her face is very calm and composed, except when (but this isn't very often now) it lights up with an excited smile. I see at last that she is just as unhappy and misses Papa just as much as I do. As I watched her the other evening, and saw her face for a moment looking quite old, I suddenly wanted to throw myself at her feet and beg her forgiveness. Is it all my fault that Papa has had to go away? But I don't think Mama means to make me feel guilty, and I know she'd be shocked if I did anything so extreme.

Paris is good for her work as well as for my schooling, and she seems pleased to be here. We live in the smart 17th arrondissement, in an elegant flat that has been lent to us by a

French publisher friend. Kiyoko has shown me where she lived with her brother when she was a student, at the same time as Papa, at the Conservatoire. It reminded me with a start that she too was once a musician. Somehow I have never been able to think of her as one: I like to see her busy with her own work. The row of books that she has translated or written (in Japanese, English, and French) has by now grown very long.

While we were in Japan I know Papa wrote at least once from Heidelberg. He is back at the Institut, and no longer playing. His instruments and the piano are in store in London. I can't bear to think of that.

I manage quite well now to be 'good and sensible' as I know he would want me to be. I am very busy. We don't have a piano here yet, so I have to go to a practice studio which we pay for. It is late when I get home. After supper there is always a heap of *devoirs* to do for the Lycée, even more than we had in London. I'm exhausted by bedtime. But it is then that I lie awake and wonder about Papa. How is he? I think about him as if I never thought about him before, and perhaps I never did. You cannot think about someone who is part of you every minute of the day; it would be like 'thinking' about music — but it's interesting that I say that, for I have just remembered how surprised I was when my new teacher, after hearing me play for the first time (I was terribly out of practice), said the same thing. He said, quite casually, 'I wonder if you have begun to think too much. That is the bad part of growing up. But you will learn to play again as everyone tells me you can, as you played as a child. Only it will be even better.'

I don't think I will ever be like a child again.

So my thinking about Papa (whom I did not need to think about) and my thinking about Mama (whom I see I ignored in the past) have somehow met in the middle.

I would like more than anything to be able to explain to them that I am all right, that things aren't so dreadful as they seem to think. I knew at once that Papa and I could not go on like that, and it must very soon be over. We had waited for one another since I was very little, it needed to happen, but we could not have continued together. I was sure of that. In a way there was no need for Kiyoko to have come home as she did. We would have grown out of ourselves! But I know it is difficult, perhaps impossible, for them to understand that, and why should they, for I see now that I had never allowed for the fact that they belonged to one another and not, first of all, to me. I would like though to believe that Papa knew it was over for me already. It might make him feel better; he could not believe we were right to be happy together. And because he was so ashamed, we hardly were. I never got the chance to tell him that it was an end, and not a beginning, and Kiyoko has made me promise not to get in touch with him. At first this was when she was very angry, but now she is calmer she says it is for his sake as well as for mine. I do not know yet what is best for her.

It helps Mama if I keep busy and do not cry any more. I cried too much in Japan. My whole aim now is somehow to make up for everything to Mama.

I suppose it was Fleur's 'Memoirs' that gave me the idea of writing these notes – I wouldn't honour them with a grander title – though I hope my notes, if ever they are read, will not give anyone such a shock as hers gave me. Mary, said Fleur, put ideas into her head. Certainly Fleur put ideas into mine! But it wasn't as simple as that exactly: it was rather that she showed me the ideas that were lurking there all the time. I really think I might never have dug them up all on my own.

(This, by the way, makes me regard with great suspicion people who say you aren't influenced by what you read: I *know* that's nonsense. And anyway, why read if it is just like rinsing out your mouth?) For although I said earlier that I had not allowed for the fact that Kiyoko and Michael belonged to one another and not to me, I had not, until I read Fleur, worked out that Papa and I could possibly think of one another in a proper grown-up way.

As I read Fleur, I felt a dreadful mixture of horror and envy. Part of me hated her for the way she seemed to have caught Papa (I couldn't really understand, though, how he could let things happen if he didn't want them to; either he did, or he didn't – I rather agreed with Fleur in those days); but the other part of me wanted to claim him for myself, to replace Fleur. And then I quickly saw how I could make him notice me differently, although, almost as I saw, I realized that he had set himself to resist me. From the day we talked on that walk, Papa did all he could to pretend not to notice me, not to hear what I was saying, not to understand what I meant. If I called to him to come and dry me after my bath, as he had always done, he would call back that he was busy; once or twice I even went deliberately to find him and handed him the towel (I must have been about twelve or thirteen by then), but he no longer wanted to help. He was irritable with me on those occasions, and I knew why. And he knew that I knew why – but he pretended that we did not know. We began to play what he had called Fleur's 'games', and Fleur's games were cruel.

He arranged for my new piano teacher to take over from him; I knew that was right, and for my sake – for right and good reasons, but because he hurried into it for wrong ones, he made it feel like treachery. He stopped coming to sit on my bed to say goodnight to me, and sometimes he even went away without letting me kiss him goodbye.

The terrible thing was that custom and circumstances were all on his side. It was only too easy for him to pretend – to lie, really – since he had simply to do the 'right thing', the thing that would surprise no one, the correct and unexceptionable thing. He became my reserved and reasonable untruthful Papa. Sometimes I was very angry with him, when for instance he would arrange with a dreadful alacrity for someone to stay in the flat 'to look after us' the minute Kiyoko went away for so much as a day. Was he afraid I would pounce on him? I learnt to conceal my feelings and quite coldly to pretend, but I despised him then for his fearfulness.

But even as I write that now, it makes me want to cry. I loved Papa far too much to be angry for long, and I never despised him. You might say that the part of me that envied Fleur lay in wait for Papa, and even fought him; but the other part, that felt a sort of horror of her, loved him better than myself and wanted to consent, saw his point of view better than my own and longed to please him. Perhaps in the end I was confused about how best I could please him. And there was not really any pleasure in finally 'catching' him, against his will, in a way he could not feel was right for us, or at least for him – which came to the same thing.

So now I want these 'notes' to be the letters to Papa that I must not write yet, or anyway, may not send. I wish I believed that by my writing he could somehow hear and understand what I am saying to him.

Papa, listen if you can! I am all right.

Summer 1982

Dear Papa, I am not very good at writing letters after all, though I think about you a great deal. Time rushes by: the

Bachot is over at last. It has been a dreadfully busy year, working for the final exams and trying to fit in my lessons at the Conservatoire and keep up my practising. We have a piano at home now which has made a great difference, and in the autumn I proceed full time to the Conservatoire.

But Papa, how I miss you! Sometimes I walk into the salon with my eyes shut; I sit down at the piano and think what I might play to you; but what would you like to hear? Schumann, Bach, Ravel . . .? I wait for your reply: I want *you* to choose. Sometimes I feel as if all the pieces I play these days are elegies. I miss you not only as an audience but as a critic too. No one has been able to replace your kind but sharp comments. Of course, my teacher is a fine critic and I listen carefully to him, but his understanding does not hit home as yours did. Increasingly I think for myself, but I still refer to you in my arguments: 'What do you think, Papa?' I long to know what you would say. I don't want to have to resort to myself to supply your thoughts and to make your choices for you, as if you were dead. How terrible it would be to be condemned to reinvent a person you loved in your own image! However hard you tried to retain him in all his exactness, slowly you would replace his tone of voice with your own; you would absorb the sound of his laugh, re-cast the slant of his mind. You could never again be surprised or disconcerted or delighted by his unpredictable response. Oh Papa! I could not bear to write your lines for you. I will think only for myself until you can speak to me in your own voice again.

Kiyoko is working on a sequence of stories with musical themes, with a Japanese artist friend who has come to live in Paris, really to be near to her. I do not want to tell you about him, Papa, though I like him and admire his work – and he was very kind to me in Tokyo – but I think you should know that Kiyoko is happier when she is with him, and so I do believe that in the long run it will be a good thing.

But now I think only of the long run.

Autumn 1982

Bonjour Papa. It is more than two years – but do I need to remind you? – since we last saw one another. I was relieved to learn from Kiyoko that you have known for some time that we are here; she had not realized I was worrying lest you had no idea where we were.

We read in the papers of the award you and von W. were given in Germany. I would like to congratulate you – I do – except that you seem to have made our lives even more dangerous. There was even a demonstration here (attended by several pupils from the Conservatoire) against the French government's acquiring your research. Aren't you greatly worried? – at least you must feel very ambivalent? We never talked about your work at the Institut: I realize it is a side of you I know nothing of. And my only personal memory of it is a very bad and trivial one: that time you were so angry with me when I interrupted you at work.

I am now full time at the Conservatoire. Apart from a few obligatory classes, and I have been asked to accompany one or two singers, I don't in fact spend much time there; mostly I am practising at home. I'm afraid there have even been complaints from our neighbours (Beethoven sonatas proved the last straw), and it is now agreed that I will not play before 8 a.m. or after 10 p.m. at night, and on Sundays not before 11 a.m. They weren't unpleasant, just rather desperate. They assure me they will all buy expensive tickets for my first recital nonetheless – whenever that great event takes place!

I realize I have hardly told you about my piano teacher

here. He too is Russian, but his playing is quite different from my first teacher's. It is warmer, more discursive, less 'pure' and delicate. I think he has already had a significant influence on my work; it has matured and relaxed. I enjoy pieces now that I can really get my teeth into, and have to grapple with intellectually, particularly at the moment Beethoven sonatas, and the *Italian Concerto*, although I can hardly play a note of the latter before someone re-opens the boring debate as to whether or not it is correct to play it on the piano.

The person who most often re-opens this debate (I say 'be quiet! just listen!') is a new friend of mine from the Conservatoire. He is called Robert -, and I tell you his name – make a note of it, Papa! – because I assure you he is one day to be a great composer. Perhaps I am a little biased in his favour, as he is already composing a piece specially for me.

A year later, autumn 1983
Papa, don't stay away much longer. I am afraid that it will become too difficult for you and Kiyoko to start again, which is what I am sure you must try to do. All this year she has been working with Y-, the artist friend I told you about. Our household has been the scene of two Artistic Collaborations: Robert is here incessantly examining me 'pianistically', as he composes his Opus One; and until July, Kiyoko and Y- sat one either side of a big table with pen and brush respectively (sometimes almost interchangeably). But in the summer he left for Japan, and Kiyoko would not go with him, although he begged her to, and for a while I thought she would. Recently I said to her that the time must have come for her to write to you, but she said she was no longer sure whether you wanted her. Nor could she tell if she really wanted you any more.

But Papa, I am sure you do; I know she does. What can I do

to make sure you both find out? I am worried now lest too much time going by will make it impossible for you to come back to one another, even to say that you want to. You mustn't let too many habits of separateness come between you. It is already three years! Be careful, Papa.

The best way for me to represent my past year to you would be simply to play a scale: Dum-de-de De-de-de-de Dum. I have practised incessantly and next June I am to be allowed to play in the leavers' Concours. After that it is already being mooted that I should make my début in March '85, around the time of my twentieth birthday. Try to be here in time to help me plan my programme.

March '84

I now look in two directions: backwards (three-and-a-half years) and forwards one year to my Paris début, which grows daily more likely.

But I also ought perhaps to admit to you that I have been ill again, just for a few weeks recently. Don't misunderstand what I am telling you, I think I just need a little longer to adjust to some new ideas. One of these ideas (which I feel you won't be surprised to hear), and the idea which upset me, really, is Robert's. He is very nice to me, when he is not rather irritatingly trying to 'civilize' me. Despite my French education he finds me lacking in general culture in all sorts of ways. He drags me round art galleries and to plays, as well as to performances of modern music by his friends. On these occasions he will hardly let me mention the piano (though he listens to me critically enough when I play), since he says I can think about that all the rest of my life.

But as I said, when he is not civilizing me (which is rather exhausting), he is very kind and gallant, almost old-fashioned,

Kiyoko says. He thinks I am 'mysterious' – but that is easily explained. I just have to be rather silent (it's usually because I have nothing to say about modern music), and look like myself, that is, Japanese.

Then suddenly he became very serious about me, and I panicked, and was ill. It's silly, but I was frightened. I can say that to you, Papa. I don't know what it will mean to love a boy – well, he is a man (he tells me so often enough), and impatient and insistent. And I'm afraid, because I don't know how I shall react to him, and whether I shall remember you too much – whether, even, I should tell him about you beforehand. And would he understand?

For I think it is 'beforehand' – only I would like to put it off for a bit longer. This worry upset me much more than I meant it to: I kept being sick, and couldn't practise properly, which is serious since the Prix is approaching. Kiyoko eventually took me away from Paris to stay in Brittany. It was very cold, but lovely there out of season. I grew calmer, and have stopped being sick.

But I *am* afraid, Papa. Tell me what I should do. Yet, whatever you say, I think I will have to tell him. It is a dreadful risk, but I don't think I can manage the other sort of risk on my own.

Later

Weeks go by. I have put off writing until I had better things to say. For we have had a very bad time, Papa. I told Robert about us: I had to; and he was dreadfully upset and shocked. I explained as much as I could, but in the end there was nothing more I could say. He said he couldn't bear to see me ever again. Then I tried to withdraw from the Prix; I didn't want to play ever again. Kiyoko and my teacher were in despair. At some point Kiyoko talked to Robert. She hadn't told me she was going to do this, but I met him running out of our house with tears streaming down his cheeks. He would not look at me. That was in April. It seemed as if there was no reason for us ever to meet again, but then, a few weeks before the Concours, he wrote to me. He said he had thought and thought about what I had said, and tried to understand my explanation, and now he felt he did. The thing he most wanted in the world was to see me again, if I could forgive him for being so harsh and selfish. It is terrible how people blame themselves. I was just wondering how I could answer this when he turned up at the flat looking like a sort of maypole; he was covered with flowers he had brought for Kiyoko and me.

For a while we were very careful of one another; we crept around rather like invalids who feel too wobbly to walk far. But he is going on with the second movement of the sonata he is composing for me. My teacher thinks it suits me and I may even perform it at the recital next year, so Robert is on tenterhooks for himself as well as for me.

Oh dear, as fast as I try to keep you up to date, everything changes. Yesterday Robert and I had a furious quarrel. I don't know how I can possibly play his piece for him. I play it as I can, as my fingers manage to read it. He says I am missing all sorts of things out that he intended. I say he hasn't put them down: they must still be in his head. One thing is certain, I can't play his sonata unless he gets on and composes it; he is only half-way through and it is very difficult to learn.

I had hardly written that when that evening Robert turned up again. He put the music back on the piano rather furtively. And now he admits he has slightly altered some of the harmonies. I was right – they were 'missing' . . .!

Then, without saying another word, he marched me firmly

into my bedroom and before I could remonstrate (even if I had wanted to) he lifted me up and put me into bed and jumped in after me. I hadn't even taken my shoes off. It was hours later and he was still there; eventually it was so late it seemed silly for him to go home at all, and so he stayed the night.

In the morning (oh, I hope I never wake up on my own again) I went to find Kiyoko to ask Robert to breakfast. I said,

'Mama, Monsieur Robert –, the mysterious composer, happens to be present and very hungry. May I ask him to breakfast?'

She was very pleased. We sat round the table laughing as if we were at a party. But now I must get back to work.

Autumn 1984

Now the Prix is behind me, all my attention is turned to the recital programme for next spring. Oh darling Papa, I had hoped you would be here by now to consult. Some Chopin, and probably Liszt (the *Sonata*) is obligatory; I am trying to choose a Beethoven sonata: I am tempted by the 'Waldstein', although practising it will probably finally alienate our long-suffering neighbours. Debussy, I think not, so that probably means Ravel: perhaps the *Tombeau de Couperin*. Then there is Robert's sonata (fifteen minutes long), and that would really be enough music, only I do want to fit in, somewhere, the *Kinderszenen*. No one, I must admit, approves of this last choice, but the more I think about it, the more I am determined to play it. My teacher advised against it, almost automatically, on the grounds that it is not interesting enough technically. But, I say, there is more than enough in the programme to demonstrate my technique: I don't want merely to show off! Schumann himself was dogged by pretentious critics who thought the *Kinderszenen* too 'childish' to be interesting. But for me it would turn my musical life full cycle; I want to include a piece that is significant in an autobiographical way, and play it to you, Papa. Without my prompting her, although I suppose she had heard me playing it, Kiyoko has already adopted the *Kinderszenen* for one of her musical tales.

Certainly Debussy's *Children's Corner* would be technically more exacting, but I don't like the pieces nearly so much.

The date is fixed at the end of March in the Salle Gaveau. It is ambitious of us to book Gaveau, but since I got a Premier Prix and Robert has his first performance which will be an added audience draw, we are advised by the agent to take the risk. We shall have to work hard if we are to fill it though. Kiyoko is drawing up a grand-sounding invitation list.

Now only you are missing, Papa. But I leave your invitation to Kiyoko.

SEVEN

Scenes of Childhood

About Strange Lands and People

Once upon a time there was a child who longed to travel. He lived in a very comfortable house, full of elegant possessions; he was given a great many toys, and there was always enough food at mealtimes. He should have been very contented. But often his mother would find him at the window, looking out at the cars going by, or gazing up at the white trail left in the clouds by an invisible aeroplane.

'I want to go away,' said the boy.

His mother was very hurt and sad. Why did he want to leave her and the rest of his family?

'You must stay here for a few more years,' she said. But because she loved him and half understood his longing, she bought him picture books which told him about distant countries and peoples. He was never happier than when he was turning their pages and imagining himself on his future travels.

Curious Story

Sometimes when he was turning the pages, the boy felt as if someone was watching him. He looked up, rather crossly, thinking his sister might have crept into the room.

'Go away,' he said, before he had even made sure.

Usually, however, there was no one there. But one day when he glanced up, the boy saw that the shiny blue china frog that sat on the mantelpiece was looking at him. The boy got up and crossed the room, and looked back in silence at the frog.

'Where do you want to go most?' said the frog suddenly.

The boy grinned.

'You decide,' he said.

'To see, or to be?' asked the frog.

The boy hesitated. He wasn't sure if he properly understood the question.

'To be, I think,' he said tentatively at last.

'Come on then,' said the frog. And he gave a huge hop that carried him right across the room on to the window sill. The boy just paused to grab his jersey, and scrambled after him.

Blindman's Buff

The frog progressed in long hops, almost as if he were flying; the boy had to run to keep up with him. They came eventually to a wood where the trees were the brightest green the boy had ever seen, so dazzling it hurt his eyes to look at them. He put up his hand to shade his eyes, and when he took it away again, the frog had vanished.

'Where are you?' called the boy, turning round and round and peering through the avenues of tree trunks. There was no answer; instead, the clatter and squawking of birds that had filled the air until then suddenly fell silent. The boy frowned. Then

'Here!' called someone. He set off down a long path through the trees towards the voice, when

'Here!' it called again, surely from the other direction. He swung round and retraced his footsteps.

'Here! Here!' The boy turned this way and that trying to decide where the voice (or was there more than one?) was coming from. The green light was fading, as if a wave of sea-water was swiftly withdrawing from the shore.

'This is stupid,' said the boy to himself, suddenly becoming impatient. 'I'm going to sit down and wait for that frog to find me. He hopped off; he can jolly well hop back.'

He sat down and waited.

Pleading Child

But the frog didn't return, and it grew darker. The boy began to feel hungry and miserable.

'Why did I follow him?' he thought angrily. 'I should have said where I wanted to go. Perhaps he would have taken me to India, or Japan. Even the North Pole would be better than just sitting under a tree on my own like this.' He searched his pockets and found a piece of chocolate. For a while he flicked through the notebook he always carried, but he hadn't got a pencil to write anything down.

The boy grew afraid. He stood up and cleared his throat and stuck his hands in his pockets.

'Frog!' he shouted. 'Where are you? Come back, it's getting late. Frog, I've got to go home!'

And as he called, a wind got up in the wood, and the branches waved and rattled as if they were a chorus echoing his words: 'Frog! Frog!' they chanted and moaned.

The boy crouched down and blocked his ears.

'Frog!' he called plaintively once more. 'Where are you?'

Perfectly Contented

'I'm here, right beside you,' was the reply. The boy jumped. He tried to hide his tears.

'You might have said so,' he snapped, for there indeed was the frog, only a few inches away from his feet. But although the boy snapped, he at once felt much better. The wind seemed to have died down as quickly as it had arisen, and the green light was once again seeping back through the higher branches.

'Where are we?' asked the boy. 'This is a funny sort of travel. I wanted to see the world, and the people who live in foreign cities.'

'Make up your mind,' said the frog. The boy hoped he would not become disagreeable so early on in their travels. 'See, or be. You said "be" when I asked you.'

'Oh!' said the boy. But he felt this was rather unfair. He had thought at the time he had not known what he was choosing.

'Trust me if you can,' said the frog more reassuringly. 'Come on, let's get going.'

The frog and the boy set off again. It was a relief to be on the move, and the boy began to enjoy himself. He even whistled a little, and tilted at the branches that got in his way.

Important Event
They came to the edge of the wood, and there ahead of them was a beautiful house, obviously quite recently built. It was made entirely of wood, and reminded the boy of pictures he had seen of houses in the Scandinavian countryside. The windows were open as if it were midsummer and perhaps it was, for butterflies and insects flew busily backwards and forwards between the garden and the house.

'Are you hungry?' asked the frog.

'Very,' said the boy. 'It would have been nearly supper time, only I saw you.'

'All right,' said the frog. 'No one can travel on an empty stomach. You can go in. They're expecting you.'

The boy perked up even more. He was sure travelling involved hospitality and meeting strangers. But then to his disappointment he saw a little girl come to the door of the house.

'Not a girl?' he said dubiously to the frog.

'Why not? You know her,' said the frog.

Where was the fun in that? But the little girl was coming towards them, so the boy resigned himself to be polite. He didn't recognize her, however, so the frog must have made a mistake. The girl put out her hand and the boy shook it.

'Hello,' he said, looking away awkwardly.

'Lunch time!' croaked the frog.

Reverie

The boy was full. He had eaten an enormous lunch, which had included freshwater trout grilled with rosemary, and a blackcurrant ice. The little girl had sat beside him, and the dishes had come and gone, he wasn't sure how. He felt like having a sleep, though it seemed rather a wasteful thing to do on such a lovely afternoon.

'I am sleepy,' he admitted to the little girl.

To his surprise she at once led him to a hammock which was slung from the strong main beam of the wooden house. They both clambered in. The door was open and the hammock rocked gently in the breeze; the buzzing of the insects seemed to grow louder and louder. The boy put his arms round the little girl to steady themselves. It was like being in a boat, anchored, but rocking as the other boats moved around the harbour. They fell asleep.

At the Fireside

Perhaps the sun had moved round and was now falling on his face, for the boy dreamt that he was standing in front of a great fireplace in a medieval hall. Whole trees burnt in the grate; the logs crackled and spat. A crowd of people, who seemed as if they had just come in from a long walk, stamped their feet noisily and warmed their hands in front of the flames.

'What are we doing?' the boy asked his neighbour, a tall man in old-fashioned clothes.

'We're waiting for' – the boy didn't catch the name – 'to come and collect your sister,' said the man.

The boy looked round. Was his sister here? And then he saw her. She was lying, straight and still, in a long green dress on a table at the other side of the hall.

He looked questioningly at the man, who simply nodded in reply. The boy went slowly across the room. He knelt down by the table, and put his arms round his sister, for it was she.

The Knight on the Rocking Horse

At that moment the doors of the hall burst open, and in rode a black knight on a huge white horse. The boy sprang up, as the horse clattered up to the table where his sister lay.

'Have you anything to say?' said the knight, in a strange accent. He did not lift the visor of his helmet. The horse blew through its nostrils and pawed the ground impatiently.

The boy felt he had a chance to say something.

'Must you take her away?' he asked.

'You must give her to me,' retorted the knight.

So the boy turned round and reluctantly scooped his sister up from the table, and lifted her up to the knight. The knight took her carefully, and held her in front of him, her face buried on his shoulder, so she did not look too uncomfortable.

'Don't go yet,' said the boy desperately, but he knew it was too late. The knight wheeled his horse round, and kicked it sharply. It leapt forward and they plunged together out of the great hall.

Almost too Serious

'Don't go!' screamed the boy, waking up and holding on to the little girl so tightly that she too woke with a dreadful start.

'What's the matter? You're hurting me!' she said, but when she saw he was crying she at once stopped protesting.

'I won't go. I'm here. What's the matter?' she said again.

'He has taken away my sister,' sobbed the boy. He no longer knew where he was or what he was doing.

The little girl looked surprised.

'Don't you recognize me?' she asked.

The boy glanced at her. He sat upright in the hammock and shouted at her.

'How can you say that? You know I've never seen you before in my life!'

But the little girl smiled up at him and moved so the hammock rocked to and fro, as if it were mocking him.

Frightening

'I want to go now,' said the boy suddenly. He began to try to get out of the hammock. 'The frog is probably waiting.'

'Oh, the frog!' said the little girl carelessly.

'Will you listen to me,' said the boy. 'I must go. Won't you let me?'

'It's not easy,' said the girl. 'Besides, you keep on looking for me. So it's the other way round really.'

'I didn't want to see you here today,' said the boy fiercely. 'I'm meant to be travelling. I want to meet new people.'

'Go then, if you can,' said the little girl. He had already swung his legs over the side of the hammock, and now he tried to heave himself up and off its swaying edge. But it lurched violently and he was thrown backwards.

'You did that,' he said accusingly. 'You're not helping. Stop swinging.'

'You must want to go,' she said.

'I think I do,' he said. 'Will you help me now?' He stopped trying to get off the hammock and looked at her. She looked back at him enquiringly.

'Don't worry,' he said. 'I'll be all right.'

He let himself flop back into the hammock, and kissed the little girl on the cheek.

'Goodbye!' he said. 'Who's taking you home?'

Child falling Asleep

When the boy had gone, the little girl lay back. She wriggled so the hammock began to swing again, and put her hands behind her head in order to think for a while. It was getting late. Unlike the boy, she didn't feel she wanted to travel any further that particular day. She realized though that she wouldn't see him again, wherever she went.

'I hope he meets interesting people on his travels,' she thought. 'But he has always been too curious for his own good.'

She felt lazy and sleepy, and before she knew where she was, she had once more fallen asleep.

The Poet Speaks

Back on the mantelpiece, the frog shook his head at the boy, that is, the pouch under his chin quivered in what seemed to be a mixture of humour and reproach.

'You made the right choice eventually,' he said. 'I hope you think so too?'

The boy smiled. It seemed to him that the frog had probably done the choosing; but yes, it had proved right.

'We can start on our real travels now,' said the frog. 'I want you to do some sensible research. Decide where you want to go. Make out an itinerary. There's all the time in the world, but we won't waste a moment. There's heaps to see! Go to bed early between now and then.'

'When?' said the boy. 'What shall I bring?'

The frog's huge eyes were closing, but one opened wide again.

'No luggage, whatever you do,' he croaked rather faintly. 'I can't stand luggage.' He grew bluer and shinier every minute as he settled back into his china skin.

EIGHT

Poste Restante

It was von W.'s wife who, in the end, handed me a pen and suggested I resume this tale. I was not anxious to hear my voice again. But Clara is a kind and sensible woman and eventually I talked a little to her. I lived in a small flat at the top of my colleague's house. At first I kept myself to myself, but by the end of a year it was assumed that I would eat at least once a week with the family, usually lunch on Sundays. They had four very young and lively children. My desire to live a solitary life could hardly prevail against Clara's generosity and the children's insouciance. Meanwhile, too, von W.'s and my work had its own remorseless momentum.

For two years I could not speak of my wife and daughter even to Clara. I had written a couple of times to Kiyoko, in order to settle affairs to do with the London flat, matters of finance, and so on, and eventually I heard from her that she and Sumi had moved to Paris, after an unsuccessful stay in Japan. I was relieved to learn of their return to Europe, and Paris seemed a good practical solution for both of them. Sumi never wrote, but in her letter Kiyoko at last gave me a little news: she said that Sumi had been ill in Japan, but was better, had a new piano teacher at the Conservatoire where she had entered at the same time as working hard for the Baccalauréat. She said absolutely nothing about herself, but once I came across a new publication of hers in a bookshop: it was a translation of Japanese tales into French, with beautiful brush drawings by an artist whose name I vaguely recalled her mentioning after one of her visits to Japan.

I had given up music entirely, but then Clara asked me if I would teach the cello to their eldest son, and it seemed churlish to refuse. He was about seven when the lessons began, and he seemed to enjoy them. But I would lie awake at night for hours afterwards.

I am ashamed to admit it – what can you possibly think of me? what can I think of myself? – but very slowly I found myself feeling better. I did not feel less guilty; the facts would never change. I blamed myself entirely for allowing myself to respond to Sumi. It was clear to me that I could have, and should have, averted the situation even at the very last minute. There was no need for things to have gone as they had. I dreaded lest she had been damaged irrevocably. But as time went by, I became, I could not help it, a little more optimistic. I somehow could not continue to believe that she would remain unhappy. Perhaps I remembered, allowed myself to remember her too well as a child, so full of life, so affectionate, that it seemed to me she could not, must not fail to recover. I had no right to think this, yet I would be deceiving myself if I did not admit that I began to feel hopeful for her, despite myself.

And so I came little by little to see that whatever problems I had made for Sumi, she was not in fact any more my problem, no longer, at least, my prime responsibility, and that my continuing crime lay in my neglect of Kiyoko, not in my past, however unforgivable, with my daughter.

I did not become complacent. Do not think I had forgiven myself. Yet I came to see there is also a complacency in self-castigation and remorse. And even, after a while, there comes a point when it is easier to luxuriate in the past than to get up and start again, which is what must be done, however much one has forfeited one's right to proceed. Clara encouraged me to think like this, to help me detect where lay the precarious middle way.

Nor was it any more a matter of tears and forgiveness. I could no longer weep as I had wept in Heidelberg seventeen years before. It was too late for that. It would have to be dry-eyed and not seeking forgiveness that I approached Kiyoko again.

That too may be hard to understand. Must I not above all seek her forgiveness? Yes, yes – and no. To seek is somehow to expect to find. I knew, with increasing sternness, that I must not wait for her to make a move or to offer anything; that it was for me to return, expecting nothing; to show her that I had returned before I had the faintest idea whether she was prepared to return to me. It was only hope that could enable me to return; but I must return without hope. All my energy was bent on achieving this equilibrium. But most of the time I shrank in horror and self-disgust at my presumption. I could not believe that Kiyoko would want to see me again. My courage failed when I remembered that terrible scene in the kitchen on the night she had come home, when, white as a ghost, she had shaken with anger as she determined on our immediate separation.

The months, the years went by, and I longed more and more to return to see her, but each time I approached anything like a resolution to go, I was overcome with shame. And then, in early January 1985, Clara came up to my flat one evening with a copy of a musical magazine that was still sent to me from London; I had never bothered to cancel the subscription that Kiyoko had taken out for me years ago, though the magazine more often than not lay around unread. I was once again at a low ebb. For the past six months I had been very restless. I slept badly, and my sleep such as it was was filled with appalling nightmares. It seemed too that even Clara had stopped trying to help me recently. I was feeling morose and sorry for myself. Clara came in and sat down and looked at me quite critically, as if I didn't deserve what she was about to say to me.

'Michael,' she said eventually, 'I have good news for you. I hope you will be pleased to see it.'

She passed me the latest copy of the magazine, and pointed to an announcement in the concerts diary. It read that on – March 1985, Mlle Sumi Inoue, who had received one of the previous year's Premier Prix at the Paris Conservatoire, would be making her début at the Salle Gaveau. But what if I had not seen it? Who had put it there? It was most unusual for a Paris concert to be advertised in the concerts diary. And Sumi had been awarded a Premier Prix!

'What if you hadn't seen it?' I demanded of Clara in horror.

'Well, I did, thank goodness,' she said.

'She is playing under Kiyoko's maiden name. It does make better sense, as names go,' I said. 'But her European training will confound expectations.'

'You will go?' asked Clara.

'It is generous of Kiyoko. She wants me to hear Sumi's recital,' I said, but wondering if that was the answer, and avoiding Clara's question for the moment. But I would go. I did not know what to expect. In February I wrote to Paris and booked myself a ticket for the Salle Gaveau.

I decided to take an overdue month off from the Institut and travel by a leisurely route through Alsace-Lorraine to Paris. I had always meant to visit Strasbourg and Nancy, two of the several universities my peripatetic grandfather had attended; the time seemed ripe for a pilgrimage. I left my car behind (although to travel by road to Strasbourg is in fact far simpler; French wives from the Institut even affected to do their shopping over the border), packed the smallest bag I had, and set off by train. As a traveller I could be content.

I was more: I was happy. Travelling, like reading, brings into play different aspects of the imagination. At one extreme the imagination operates as a process of recognition; the deeply familiar is uncovered and at the same time transformed, and made new. At the other extreme, the imagination succumbs to the charms of the unfamiliar, the exotic, the apparently new. The first is not to be despised as a limited and traditional exercise, although it carries the risk of degenerating into nothing more than a process of self-identification. Ideally it is much more, and represents the discovery of everything from which the mere self sprang, and to which it may return, to which it may give back itself. It is a two-way process, or it is nothing. It could perhaps be described as an essentially conservative, or even domestic, form of imagination; but it is not only weariness that takes us home.

In Alsace, even as the conservative in me responded to the entirely familiar surroundings, I also became aware of my long dormant craving for the rare, the exotic. I found the particular mixture that is Strasbourg comfortable, recognizable, good-humoured, and domestic. The furniture that I sat on, the glasses I drank from, and even the curious mixture of languages (in the street it seemed as if no single sentence finished in the language in which it began) expressed almost exactly the mixture I had found in the past in my grandparents' house, though perhaps without quite the degree of French elegance; that had taken its flavour from the capital. At weekends in Heidelberg, I would be ensconced in my laboratory, and apart from the von W.s', I had observed little of the domestic routine of the inhabitants. On Sunday morning in Strasbourg the town seemed to burgeon with families, and for several hours I felt I was witnessing a vision of domestic harmony. The arrival of each family on the scene (a playground by the river in the pedestrian quarter of old Strasbourg) would be heralded by the oldest boy on a bicycle, who entering like a bull into the ring would swerve to a halt, spraying sand over an incautious bystander. He would be followed by his sister, and she invariably carried, perched unhappily on the back wheel of her bicycle, a younger child who, clinging round his or her sister's accommodating but wayward waist, protested shrilly. Finally came the sedate parents, the father in Sunday coat and hat, with a fourth child, the infant, in sling or pram. They would traverse the playground in a ritual progress as their children wheeled and curvetted around them, until they all vanished round the corner on their way home for lunch – or perhaps to have their family portrait painted.

Of course, if I looked at individuals more specifically I could detect that the *pères de famille* were quite harassed and even a little bored by the antics of their carefree children, and the mothers, welcoming the rest from the solitary responsibility of the week, appeared unnaturally complacent and abstracted. But there was (I thought it was not only in myself) a pervading feeling of contentment, expressed in the generally mild and peaceful faces and gentle play. Only the haunting cries of the seagulls which had flown up river and now swooped over the weirs and bridges of the Ill reminded one that there was a pressure of movement elsewhere. And then I saw a family who stood out from the rest as an Expressionist portrait might from a Dutch family interior. They had an alien, almost gipsy-like beauty: the mother, thin, with long rather wild dark hair, wore a high-waisted black coat and soft Russian boots, and her daughter, perhaps ten or eleven years old, was a perfect miniature version of her. Both were rather insubstantial and distraught, a little *effrayées*. Hand in hand, they appeared to be blown rather than to walk across the bridge on which I passed them. They were accompanied by a man, presumably the husband and father, for whom I felt such a violent pang of envy that I turned away and clutched at the parapet.

I was aware from then on of a sort of anguish at the heart of my contentment. But I remained outwardly relaxed. The weather varied from hour to hour, almost from minute to minute, as the year fumbled between winter and spring. Sometimes it was bright, blue-skied and sunny and one could sit for quite long stretches on benches along the riverside, although patches of snow still lay unmelted on the steeply-pitched north-facing roofs and cobbled pavements. Then the sky would darken abruptly and it rained harshly; sometimes it clouded over for a whole day. Those times I spent inside, in bars or more reluctantly, when I steeled myself to cross the threshold, in museums. In Colmar, however, I spent a long time admiring the Grünewald *Retable d'Issenheim*, and found that my taste had after all developed since the days when I had stared unfeelingly at the *Pietà d'Avignon*.

And so, while I drifted as I had not done since those student years, and basked in the smoke-filled university cafés of Nancy and Strasbourg (places I would never normally have entered), my thoughts, like an army preparing to invade, mustered themselves.

Two days before I was due to move on to Paris, I took myself out to supper to celebrate my fiftieth birthday in what had quickly become my favourite restaurant. I had sat there late, reading, on several occasions, and the *patron* had seemed pleased rather than irritated by my long, not particularly, from his point of view, profitable sojourns (nor did he object to my pipe). But on this evening my book was to remain unopened since the moment I arrived and installed myself in a corner with a good view of the room, I noticed, sitting on her own at a nearby table, an attractive youngish French woman (I supposed she was about thirty). I found myself wondering whether I should not try to talk to her. I was quite tired of my own company by now, but I have never really found that it is possible to meet someone out of the blue, let alone (since my thoughts were racing) to pick someone up, who could prove sympathetic. The margin of error seems so very great, and my successes in this field had been in the past extremely limited. For the last few years, moreover, I had lived like a monk. It has always amazed me that people can, apparently, out of peremptory necessity, combine so easily, seemingly oblivious of all the many things that may come between them. I have only felt instantly attracted to and so brave enough to approach some three or four people in my whole life; the rest came about as a matter of accident, or thanks to a context in which the preliminary sorting had somehow taken place, often done by others, and in which I was, more or less, a parasite. In these I had as it were sent a runner ahead of me who had returned with reassuring news. But in the case of Kiyoko, I had, I am glad to say, played my own advance guard.

The thought then of crossing all the boundaries of acquaintanceship, regardless of history, of past and future; the necessity of trusting oneself to the mere present presence of a person, usually fills me with horror. The scope for embarrassment, mortification, and dislike seems boundless. Even if the chemistry of affinity were no more than a matter of smell: how could you know you would like a stranger's smell? (And, to leave aside for a moment one's own incalculable reactions, it is not even total strangers whose behaviour you cannot predict in close proximity: women who have slightly bored you, even got on your nerves with too much talk, however intelligent, may become delightfully peaceful once you are marooned with them in bed: silent, they grow beautiful. The contrast is acute and correspondingly desirable. On the other hand, witty and seemingly worldly and competent women may become surprisingly awkward and ill at ease; it is as if their agility of mind is left behind with their clothes, and you feel as uncomfortable about them as you feel when you see a racehorse lying on the ground: simply, it does not look right! An elegant and correct person may reveal a glaring banality of behaviour in bed, resorting to clichés and coynesses and vulgarities of word and action that are not at all in tune with her normal style. A girl you had not thought of as particularly graceful, even rather clumsy or cumbersome, when she no longer has to contend with gravity becomes subtle and adaptable, rather as a fat person, sustained by the rhythm of the music, may suddenly prove an excellent dancer. All these surprises, good and bad, do not, however, reveal the 'essential' person, as if in the process of love-making a cloak of deception falls away, baring the 'best' and the 'worst'; on the contrary, they may be mere inconsistencies which do or do not find sympathetic accommodation. At worst physical passion tends to blur all these distinctions in a sort of blind rummage. The best you can hope for is to recognize someone in bed, and to like them better afterwards. More – or less – would follow in time.)

Perhaps the reserved conservative nature thwarts itself by insisting on protecting itself from the perils of the unknown. Yet I cannot help but feel that the circumspection of social ritual and formulae is designed to help one move with greater ease and grace; such decorum does not merely stem from fear of the alien, but also out of a distaste for the absurdities, the inappropriateness of the random.

And yet... one may be beguiled. (How, even, be beguiled were it not from an established formal position?) And so, even as I was theorizing to myself in this hypocritical and priggish fashion, I was actually glancing at the young woman when she wasn't looking, and she, it soon occurred to me, was glancing at me when she thought I wasn't looking. Eventually our looks coincided; we both returned with renewed interest to our respective concerns, I to my study of the menu, she to the arrival of her first course. If I looked again, and ventured a cautious, far from importunate smile? It did seem as if our actions, if not conspiring, were at least corresponding. She now afforded me a tentative, far from flirtatious smile in return. Oh God! Was I to proceed like an accomplished seducer? At this point I almost scowled at her in desperation and she, looking a little perplexed, began her attack on a large bowl of *moules*. But now fortune intervened (I don't think I would have got much further on my own, and my book lay temptingly to hand); one of her *moules* shot out of her grasp and landed, like a gift from the gods, almost at my feet. This was a great relief to both of us. We burst out laughing; I retrieved the *moule* and, though it did not seem quite necessary to return it to her plate, plucked up courage to ask her if she recommended them (they are one of my favourite dishes, and may have done something to ensure that the 'smell' of the evening was auspicious).

'Mais oui, elles sont très bonnes,' she replied in a lively voice, and in a Parisian accent which it was a pleasure to hear. French in these regions seemed to have entirely escaped the jurisdiction of the Academicians. I grew resolute.

'I suppose you would not consider joining me?' I asked. 'In fact you could help me celebrate my birthday. It seems a little sad . . .' and I waved my hands.

She hesitated. I looked rather vague. (Perhaps I had gone too far? 'Sad' sounded too emotional, a bit desperate?)

'Well, why not?' she said. (After all, I don't look like a Don Juan, but like a middle-aged professor.) 'It would be a pleasure.'

I called the *patron* and asked him to effect the convergence of our *couverts*, and this was done in the twinkling of an eye and with the utmost naturalness. I had been right to appreciate this restaurant. We deliberated over a rather special bottle of wine.

The next few minutes, which may prove to be fraught with difficulties as your worst fears are realized, went very easily. In France there is always the cuisine to discuss, and it is a far more productive subject than the weather. I rather ungraciously bemoaned the Alsatian food I had been eating the past few days, just tantalizingly French enough to make one pine for the real thing. We agreed it was simply not possible to find a properly cooked omelette; they arrived like synthetic sponges sinking under the weight of the ubiquitous stones of ham. But, 'Ce n'est pas grave lorsqu'il y a des moules comme ça!'

The excellent *moules*, in their fragrant and sea-watery sauce, took up their fair share of time and attention.

'Well, fifty, I fear,' I admitted eventually, in answer to her question. She didn't seem to think this was beyond the pale; she was thirty-two.

'Not married?' I enquired.

'Not married. And you?'

I outlined the uncertainties of the situation, and she seemed to appreciate them in a matter-of-fact but not insensitive way.

With a liqueur, and then a second, stood us by the *patron* – who by now, I couldn't help noticing, was rather too obviously enjoying the success of his Pandarus-like role: I hoped it wouldn't put her off – the birthday party grew ever more festive, and quite soon we were walking a rather erratic path home together, arm in arm, along the canal and then the river – that is, I was accompanying her home, which was the only gallant thing to do considering she was my guest for the evening. But with curiously little fuss I continued with her up to coffee in her room. She had a tiny apartment high up under one of the steep roofs; it must have been behind the third row of *lucarnes*. The ceilings sloped so acutely that I could hardly stand without hitting my head. It was obviously sensible to sit down as quickly as possible.

At first we made love in the frame of mind in which we had talked, quite matter-of-factly, and with the sort of enquiring courtesy that makes humorous allowance for the small blunders of unaccustomed contact. It is a privileged form of love-making (exploratory, intelligent) in which lust is not absent (the smell, the taste of *moules*) but modified by a lightly granted friendship of the moment, an entirely unexplained sense of trust and ease.

Later in the night, constrained by the uncomfortably narrow bed and waking up too hot and with cramped shoulders, I woke her deliberately and we made love again, but this time both of us more selfishly and insistently. Marie cried out in my ear like one of the seagulls I had heard calling over the Strasbourg bridges. The cries of women making love have always filled me with a mixture of tenderness and fear; I stroked her anxiously to reassure myself as much as to calm her. Then I fell into a deep sleep.

In the morning, when I opened my eyes, she was sitting on the edge of the bed apparently waiting for me to wake up. I put out my hand and traced the shape of her mouth until she pushed my tickling finger away. So then I sat up (bumping my head on the ceiling) and kissed her instead.

'I have to go to school,' she said, 'and I can't really leave you here.'

This seemed over-scrupulous in one who had cried out like a seagull and whose mouth still tasted of *moules*.

'Be late for once. I hope it is "for once"?' I said, pulling her back into bed, and I'm afraid she must anyway have been late for her pupils that day.

'Come back if things don't work out,' said Marie, as we parted at the foot of her narrow stairs. It was a cheering thought, and I hope we both felt the better for it.

By the time I reached Paris I had already become much more subdued. Anticipation, which I fought against, a sense of anticlimax as I arrived and claimed my hotel room, the thought of the unplanned week ahead of me – it suddenly seemed far too long – before the day of Sumi's recital, all contrived to make me feel utterly exhausted. I lay like a stone on my bed that evening, did not go out for supper, and slept in late the next morning.

The first thing I had to do in Paris was to buy a few clothes. I must have been very distracted to think I could manage with the little I had with me. I was rather extravagant, and enjoyed trying on some expensive (but comfortable) shoes, and even bought a new suit. I looked at my appearance critically for the first time in years: my hair was much greyer but as thick as ever; I had put on some, but not a great deal, of weight (I still took the same size in collars). After a day or two, however, I took off my new clothes and got back with relief into my old ones which by now had returned, pressed and revived, from the cleaners.

My arrival coincided with the sudden decision of the season to commit itself; the trees burst into blossom overnight; freshly-painted tables and chairs appeared on the pavements, and optimistic visitors risked the brief showers and cold gusts of wind in the attempt to prove to themselves and to the more sceptical Parisians that it was indeed spring. Notices of Sumi's recital covered the boards outside the Salle Gaveau, and occasionally bobbed up elsewhere; the agent had worked hard at the publicity. My head began to resound with the scales that somewhere nearby Sumi must be practising. One morning I wandered into the Madeleine and by chance found a rehearsal of the *John Passion* in progress. The music threw me into a state of nervous exhilaration and I listened with a sort of fascinated envy to the gamba soloist. But what was there to stop me picking up an instrument myself, oh, not professionally any more, but to play? For the first time I wondered anxiously about the instruments in store in London: how would they have survived these years of neglect?

I walked everywhere, as I had in Alsace, and saw more of Paris in that week than I had seen during the whole year I spent there as a student. I resisted only going to my favourite park, the Parc Monceau, as I thought it was too near Kiyoko's address for comfort. I did not want to cause her embarrassment. But two days before the recital I did go there; I walked rapidly through the park early in the morning, as the gardeners were opening it up and raking the paths; and saw Sumi.

She was walking slowly along the main avenue, holding hands with a tall young Frenchman, who was leaning over her and, at the moment I caught sight of them, turning her face towards his with his forefinger. I went on walking towards them, but did not slow down as we drew level. Sumi glanced away from the boy as we passed; she saw me, controlled her start of amazement, smiled, and at the same time, as I almost hesitated, left me in no doubt that I should not stop then. I walked on, and was already leaving the park before I turned round to see if what I thought I had seen was true. Sumi and the boy were just disappearing round the far corner.

But she was right: I must see Kiyoko first. What, though, was I to do about this? How had I left this most important decision so late in the week? I sat the rest of the morning in a bar trying to decide what would be best. Should I just turn up at the recital, and meet her in public on Sumi's great day? I began to think that wasn't right; I should see her on her own, independently of the ostensible reason for my coming to Paris. But then, should I ring her up? It seemed so casual. Write to her? I had already left it too late to do that. Should I simply go round to the flat and ring the bell? But someone else might be there. Even Sumi might be in (was she still living there?) and I did not want that. And besides, it would be to assume too much. I looked longingly at the door of the bar. But this was not Heidelberg all those years ago.

At three o'clock I rang the flat and Kiyoko answered; but I panicked and put the receiver down. After all (I now contradicted myself), if she had given me any indication – and it may not have been she – it was only to put the announcement of Sumi's recital in a magazine I might well not have seen. At the very best, she might still welcome the formality and protection of a public meeting. It would be possible then for me to tell whether she wanted to see me again or not. I did not really know any more whether this was the reasoning of cowardice, or of concern for her. Would the interval of the concert itself be time enough? But then she would surely be surrounded by other people, or she might even disappear backstage to see Sumi. Nevertheless, this is what, after much tortuous debate, I determined on.

The day before the recital I went firmly to a library and installed myself at a desk to read a pile of recent papers on my subject. I read hard and usefully for about seven hours, only going out once for a coffee, and by the evening had filled an exercise book with notes and jottings, half drafted a lecture, and felt pleasantly tired. I requested some photostats to be made and sent to von W. Then I gave myself supper in a small restaurant near to my hotel; as I ate a perfectly cooked omelette I relaxed almost to the point of wishing that Marie could be there to appreciate it.

The minutes before a recital are not like those before an orchestral concert or an opera. Then the hall is filled with the squeaks and grunts of wind instruments, low premonitory rumbles from the timps, and the blatant scrapings of tuning strings; a cheerful anarchy prevails. But now, isolated on the platform, there stands a solitary and silent piano, and I knew that isolated, offstage, the soloist waited in her lonely dressing room. If it is harrowing before one of your own recitals, it is even worse, I decided, before your daughter's début. An attendant came on and opened the lid of the piano to its full height; the seats in the hall were slowly filling. The Salle Gaveau is large for a début, but the publicity and presumably Kiyoko's invitations had done their work: there would not be many empty seats. I moved restlessly in my place, and looked round, at this door and that, to see if I could find Kiyoko.

She came in, at the very last minute, on the arm of the young Frenchman I had seen with Sumi in the Parc Monceau. She looked incredibly beautiful: older – a little; more elegant than any woman I have ever seen before or since. I found I had forgotten the particular angle at which she held her head; it was a mixture of proud (the chin) and modest (the eyes), the effect both vulnerable and yet not to be presumed upon. The young man showed her to her seat with old-world decorum, helped her off with her cloak which he put over the empty seat next door to them, and sat down beside her. I could still just see her face as she turned to talk to him.

It was all I could do not to leave the hall and go back to Heidelberg there and then.

Belatedly I began to consider the programme Sumi had chosen. The programme for a début is designed with several specific things in mind. The new performer, moving proudly on to the well-trodden stage, must show his power to compete with what has been done in the past and also demonstrate what he can do that is better and new. He will, therefore, choose a mixture of traditional works that put him in direct competition with his predecessors, at once displaying his technical virtuosity and testing his originality of interpretation, and of works that will mark out the area he has already made and (if it is a true choice) will continue to make his own.

Sumi's programme admirably filled these requirements. The first half was long, but well-balanced, and consisted of Ravel's *Tombeau de Couperin*, the Chopin *Barcarolle*, and the athletic 'Waldstein' sonata. The second half was courageous (and would make sure the critics remained in their seats) in that it began with the first performance of a Sonata by an unheard-of French composer; she was to finish in exemplary style with the Liszt *Sonata*, the playing of which at the end of this taxing and if anything over-long programme would above all demonstrate her stamina. But before the Liszt there was a piece that gave me pause, in that it is never really considered as material for virtuoso performance (if the press had lasted this long, they would surely depart now), and also was a particularly unlikely choice for a young performer. Schumann's *Kinderszenen* may certainly be a test of the delicacy of style and imagination in a mature player, and of course they are charming played by children. But in the years between? However, Sumi had not, so far as I could remember, played them as a child, and I was interested to see what she would make of them.

It was the young Frenchman who, seeing me hovering at the edge of the group surrounding them, and seeming to think he recognized me, introduced my wife to me in the interval that evening.

'May I present to you Mme Inoue, but now, forgive me, I realize I do not know your name?' he said. I kissed her hand.

'This,' said Kiyoko, and I noticed she put her other hand on his shoulder, as if to comfort him in advance for the foolishness of his introduction, 'is my husband, Dr Michael—.'

Then she said to him (for he had flinched despite her kindness),

'Robert, you must hurry if you are going to see Sumi. Give her our love, and tell her the "Waldstein" went better than she had expected. I'm sure you have some last-minute instructions to give her!'

Then I understood he was the composer of the piece that was to receive its first performance in the second half. But now, as he left, I turned back to Kiyoko, whose hand I still held.